LEAD
WITH
LOVE

**A Guide to Organizational Leadership
That Starts with You**

LEAD
WITH
LOVE

**A Guide to Organizational Leadership
That Starts with You**

by

Stephen Juracka Ed.D

eBooks2go
Your Author Journey Begins Here

Quantity Purchases:
Companies, professional groups, clubs, and other
organizations may qualify for special terms when ordering
quantities of this title.
For information, email info@ebooks2go.net,
or call (847) 598-1150 ext. 4141.
www.ebooks2go.net

Published in the United States by eBooks2go, Inc.
1827 Walden Office Square, Suite 260, Schaumburg, IL 60173

ISBN: 978-1-5457-5533-4

Library of Congress Cataloging in Publication

Contents

CONTENTS

Introduction

As we look across the historical landscape of our communities, our county, and the globe, there is no shortage of great leaders who have set examples for us to carry forth. The greatest leaders among us have always cast a vision of hope and called us to action. They ask us to take charge in making our corners of the world just a bit better and they stand on a platform of deep conviction and purpose. They are driven to inspire their view of a better world into existence.

The greatest leaders are not the ones who pretend to be perfect but those who walk in genuine humility while willing to do the hard work, lead by example, and who give of themselves to enrich the lives of others. Whether in family, business, politics, or in our public institutions, the impact leaders make is crucial to the well-being of our organizations and communities. **A leader's ability to live out their mission, to establish the right culture and climate, to create effective systems and efficiencies, and to design for success is often the linchpin for organizational effectiveness.**

Many of us have had the experience of working with, or for, leaders who lack savvy in leading and influencing others. At times you may have felt the sting of a leader who lacks organizational skill, a sense of direction, clear expectations, or has an inability to connect and/or relate to others. Further, you may have had the unfortunate experience of being impacted by a leader who lacks integrity or a moral aptitude and asks you to do as they say but not as they do. Unfortunately, we observe these types of traits and characteristics all too often in our politicians, our business leaders, and the people we entrust with our communities.

While there are plenty of poor leadership examples in our current cultural climate, there are also many great examples. These examples have been studied and researched, allowing us to extract their nutrients for our own growth and positioning us to exemplify great leadership in our own spheres of influence. There needs to be a call to action whereby we seek to promote leadership that is high minded and effective, which also serves to create goodness, completeness, and connectedness among us. We need leaders who are personally healthy, socially in tune, emotionally astute, and who display a deep sense of meaning, purpose, and self-awareness in their work. Let there be no mistake: Leaders like this exist everywhere. They lead their families, they serve in their churches, they lead in the boardroom, and they coach winning teams. It is time for us to elevate and emulate leaders who serve, who develop others, who are driven, and who succeed from a place of personal strength, mindfulness, and dedication to both loving themselves and others.

The goal of this book is simple: create better leaders by supporting personal health and well-being, empowering them to bring their internal strength to their seat of leadership. The objective is to share the research around personal and organizational well-being while sharing examples of quality leadership that are steeped in love of self and others.

In nearly every major religion, there is one basic principle: to love your neighbor, no matter their background, as you are to love yourself. This book is dedicated to that principle. As leaders, we are responsible for those with whom we have been entrusted, and we are also responsible for living our best lives by creating the best possible model of ourselves. As models, it is imperative that we take ownership in constructing ourselves for ourselves, but also design ourselves so as to provide great value to others and our organizations.

The adage "you can't pour from an empty vessel" should remind us that as leaders our cups must be full. We need to have designed ourselves to be individuals who step into the arena as whole and complete. We must be individuals who are in a state of peace and contentment, who have created the right environments in our own lives to support our happiness and growth for the purpose of then being able to pour ourselves out onto our families, our colleagues and those we lead. When our vessels are full, we are able to bring a positive energy and spirit to our work that is contagious and resonant. When we lead from a place of energy, positivity, and enthusiasm, our ability to impact others will resonate, and our light will shine on others. Research in the field of positive psychology will attest, happy people are more effective. Success does not breed happiness; rather, happiness breeds success.[1] When our vessels are full, we will have a greater impact in building and sustaining those we lead.

I want to pause here and add to the basic premise of this book: Effective organizations embody high engagement, a strong sense of collaboration, ownership among members, and provide autonomy and agency to the people in the organization.[2] Leaders who support such environments recognize that in order to do so they must be willing to give of themselves for those in the organization. An authoritative, top-down approach, which may be effective for a time, will not provide the love and care needed to support a sustainable and effective organizational environment. Not to mention, authoritarianism does not provide the lifeblood for allowing others to prosper and give back to the mission of the organization. Therefore, if we want to lead from a place of love, we have to be complete individuals who recognize the need to give to others, develop others, and create the right emotional climate for others to thrive and flourish. Too often leaders will overlook the importance of creating an environment that allows employees to flourish. This book is written to promote personal well-being for the purpose of creating leaders who will support organizational environments of collaboration, engagement, and personal agency.

Jim Collins, in his best-selling book *Good to Great*, explains that successful leaders are highly motivated and driven while displaying a sense of personal humility. They put the organization before themselves in order to achieve the purpose and mission of

[1]Shawn Achor, *The Happiness Advantage: How a Positive Brain Fuels Success in Work and Life* (New York: Currency, 2010).
[2]Kim Farris-Berg and Edward J. Dirkswager, *Trusting Teachers with School Success: What Happens When Teachers Call the Shots* (Lanham, MD: R&L Education, 2012).

the organization[3]. On the contrary, for many, leadership is about personal success and using others to promote themselves and their personal agendas. We see this play out all too often in our businesses, schools, and political arena. Politicians and elected officials use their political office for personal and monetary gain while leaving their moral principles at the door. In business around the United States, we see countless examples of theft and corruption in which people in authority disgrace the trust they have been given and serve to damage people and organizations for their own selfish gain. Further, we have witnessed countless cover ups and secrecy from the highest-ranking officials in some of our religious institutions. Our religious leaders have attempted to sweep atrocities under the rug to avoid their own personal and organizational humiliation. Even in our places of worship, which are supposed to provide a moral foundation for our communities, do we see a lack of love and care for people and the ones they are intended to serve. And while these examples of selfishness and moral degradation exist, this is a call for hope, service, humility, and love in every seat of leadership in every church, school, and business.

It is important that the golden rule is still the rule in today's organization and that as leaders we approach our work with a high sense of morality, integrity, and, yes, love for people. Leaders need to step into the arena with the intent of creating better lives for the people they employ and for the customers they serve.

No matter the arena, we have a tremendous opportunity and responsibility to serve to make the lives of others better. Twenty years ago, when I taught in our public schools, my mission was simple: create an environment to help kids become a better version of themselves. Today my mission isn't much different. I still seek to create environments that allow people to make themselves better. My practice may be a bit more skilled, and experiences may have changed me, but after over two decades of research and leadership experience, I know that when we set up an environment founded in love, we create an environment in which people thrive and flourish.

---

[3]Jim Collins, *Good to Great: Why Some Companies Make the Leap ... and Others Don't* (New York: HarperCollins, 2009), 102–105.

Leading with love is about loving yourself and developing yourself for the purpose of loving and developing others to, in turn, create better lives and organizations.

After twenty-two years in education, I am inspired to teach, to grow, to learn, and to be an open source for those of us who are driven to lead with purpose, compassion, and for the greater good of our neighbors. My work in education has afforded me the opportunity to research, to coach, and to lead with genuine compassion. I have led countless teams, driven a multitude of educational initiatives, coached teachers to lead, served communities, driven strategic plans, and have always sought to lead from the seat I was in with mindfulness and effectiveness. I have and will continue to be driven to create an environment for my employees that allows them to come to work highly motivated and leave at the end of the day with a sense of fulfillment.

I am excited to share *Lead with Love* with those who take up their torch every day, not only for themselves but also for those they lead. This work is grounded in research related to leadership, positive psychology, organizational change, and organizational psychology. I am inspired to share a perspective of leadership that is grounded in the most powerful and inspirational source that exists for human beings: *love*. Love is the greatest source of kindness, compassion, care, and commitment, and it is the foundation of nearly all modern spiritual belief systems. And while this book is not intended to be a religious experience, it is intended to reach the core of our humanity and explore leadership topics through the lens of love for self and others.

As we dig deeper into this journey together, know this experience is designed to promote personal growth and love of self in order to bring our best selves to the office, the home, or to our communities. The premise is that when we lead from a place of wholeness and high-mindedness we are better able to serve, to build, and to get it done.

This book is intended to cover both personal and organizational well-being in a simple manner that allows each person to be able to apply the concepts to their own person, story, and leadership position.

This book is designed to be easily understood and transferable to all arenas. I believe that keeping things simple allows us to execute more effectively and this book intends to carry out that belief.

No joy can equal the joy of serving others.

—*Sai Baba*

Part I

In part I, we will look at the importance of purpose and meaning in our lives and how that impacts our mindset for leadership. We will examine the importance of servant minded leadership and ways in which we contribute to the lives of others. We will explore the regular habits and routines that support our own personal well-being and what it means to be intentional about our own fulfillment.

Part II

Part II will focus on employee engagement, creating purpose, and developing meaning for the people we lead and our organization. We will cover the importance of creating strong teams and look at the ingredients for motivating our teammates. Part II will explain the elements of organizational well-being that foster greater personal and physiological connections within an organization. Finally, part II will conclude with the importance of adult learning and mentorship, and the importance of investing in those we lead.

Part III

In part III, we will look to take a systems approach to caring for our organizations. Being systematic and intentional about how, and who, we hire is a game changer in creating an excellent team and organization. Further, we will dive into developing strong teams who have the right tools to execute and hit their targets. Finally, we will leap into taking an aerial view of our teams and organizations to manage and leverage change.

As Sai Baba states above: "No joy can equal the joy of serving others." Serving others is not always easy. Investing in our own lives and the lives of others is hard, it is challenging, but it will bring joy and fulfillment to our lives. Please know that *Lead with*

Love is not a fragile approach to being a leader. Rather, *Lead with Love* is tough, takes personal determination, drive, and a heightened sense of intentional focus. When we lead with love, we take the steps to strengthen ourselves, those we lead, and the organizations we care for. When we lead with love, we are doing the hard work to make our corners of the universe a better place for our neighbors and ourselves.

PART I

Loving and Caring
for Ourselves

Chapter

Living Your Purpose

Your purpose in life is to find your purpose and give your whole heart and soul to it.

—Buddha

As humans, we are complex and dynamic beings who are continuously growing and developing throughout our lifetimes. Our road to maturation takes longer than any other living animal, and we are completely dependent on one another in ways that are far beyond just our basic needs. With such deep interconnectedness and dependence on one another it is important that we care for ourselves in order to bring our best selves to others and the larger community. We each play an integral role in strengthening our society and we must be sure to take responsibility for our personal health and well-being.

You'll notice when flying a commercial airline all flights start with the flight crew walking us through the safety procedures, which include how to manage the loss of cabin pressure. The directions always incorporate putting your oxygen mask on first! Why?

Because you have to be able to care for yourself before you can begin helping others. The same is true in life, in our homes, in our schools, in our businesses and in our communities. We need to put our mask on first. If we expect to lead without taking care of ourselves first, we are not going to be able to support those who need us and who rely on us for support. If we are trying to lead without first loving ourselves, we may be operating without our oxygen masks.

Recently, I was leading a five-person team designed to support the teaching and learning of close to three thousand students. We were a team with a lot of demands, and we were expected to accomplish more than we were probably resourced to execute; however, we fired on nearly all cylinders, and we were knowledgeable, efficient, and top performers on many accounts. As a team of highly skilled and highly willed performers, we were accustomed to the long hours and heavy demands. But after driving so hard for so long we recognized that we needed to take some significant time for self-care, or our team would burn out. As a team, we were dedicated to the habits and rituals that would recharge our batteries, with the exception of just one individual. And while she was a top performer in so many areas, she did not take intentional moments for self-care. She kept driving and driving with the idea that self-care was selfish and weak. Simply put, she felt she didn't have time. **I will put this simply: If you are too busy for self-care, you are too busy. You need to prioritize time for you.**

After about two years of performing at this burning pace she broke down. She was emotionally exhausted, her professional relationships were suffering, and she was not able to bring her best self to the office because there wasn't much left of her. Her ability to deal with conflict was spent. She was devoid of patience and her department suffered. Her department suffered not because she didn't have the knowledge, experience, or skills. It suffered because she was not able to bring her complete self to the work. Her ability to connect, care for others and find joy had been lost and sacrificed for unrelenting drive and production.

Research would attest, that while life offers plenty of work to those of us who are driven and motivated, we will perform our

best when we bring our complete selves steeped in care and love. In part I, we will walk through some of the habits, rituals, routines, and practices that will support us in being our best selves every day. These practices will support us being the best leaders we can be in our homes, offices, and community.

On several occasions, I have been asked by my employees why am I always smiling in the office. As I write this, just as recently as yesterday, one of my project managers asked me, "What are you smiling about?"

And while my short answer was jokingly, "I'm living the dream," it is because I have and feel I have deep meaning, purpose, and the beauty of *hope* in my life and in my work. And while the circumstances of life are certainly not all cotton candy and rainbows, I know my *why* and think deeply and mindfully about the human experience.

It is my hope that, unlike the colleague I mentioned above, you recognize that self-care is the foundation of bringing your best self to the arena. I hope you are thirsty for wanting a better life for yourself and the people you impact; and you recognize that you are designed for loving yourself. As much as we are not in control of the many things that affect our lives—that is, aging, other people's emotions, traffic, diminishing hairlines, and the list goes on and on—we are in control of the mindset, habits, rituals, and practices we establish in our lives. Mountains of research will support that if we intentionally practice implementing positive routines and habits we will experience a better life for ourselves.

Starting with Why

As humans we are wired for meaning and purpose. It drives us, and it leads us to accomplish and serve.[4] Meaning and purpose lead us to be happier people with more complete and joyful lives.[5] Whether we are driven to be the best fathers we can be, great coaches, motivational teachers, or the tastiest chef, we are formed for purpose

[4]Daniel H. Pink, *Drive: The Surprising Truth About What Motivates Us* (New York: Penguin Press, 2011).
[5]Martin Seligman, *Flourish: A Visionary New Understanding of Happiness and Well-Being* (New York: Simon and Schuster, 2012).

5

and accomplishment. So, what is your why? What is your meaning and purpose for your actions and your life? Although this question might be seemingly I, it is wildly important. Stephen Covey[6] and Simon Sinek[7] would both attest that this is where we start. We need to be proactive about our why. Our why gives meaning and purpose to our lives. It gives us energy and power to produce and create. It charges our batteries to achieve, and it gives us a goal for which to strive. Our why is our starting point for creating our end game. Friedrich Nietzsche says it this way: "He who has a why to live can bear almost any how."

I have been interviewing candidates for fifteen years, and when I conclude most interviews I typically ask the candidate if they have any questions for me. I know—not earth-shattering! On occasion, however, candidates will ask me why I do what I do. Ironically, just like I mentioned earlier, it goes back to my purpose. I want to help people become better people and make the lives of others better. That's it. I may be accomplishing my purpose in my line of work, but it is not the line of work that is my purpose. My line of work is a conduit for accomplishing my purpose. I could accomplish my purpose not only in education but in my home, in my business ventures, or even on the golf course—although I don't recommend you trying to be a golf coach unless you have the credentials; that's serious business!

When we are clear about our *why*, our work will have greater purpose, and if our *why* is founded in the core of humanity, it will lead to a richer and more meaningful life. When we care for ourselves, we seek to bring joy and happiness into our lives. Knowing *our why* gives us deeper meaning leading to improved happiness.

Have you taken a moment to reflect on your *why*? Have you written down what it is you bring to the world every day? If this is a foreign concept, you must take some time to quiet yourself and ask what you

[6]Stephen R. Covey, *The 7 Habits of Highly Effective People* (New York: Free Press, 2004).
[7]Simon Sinek, *Start with Why: How Great Leaders Inspire Everyone to Take Action* (New York, Penguin Press, 2009).

want to be known for? To illustrate, I would ask you to imagine your retirement party. Imagine your spouse, your parents, your kids, your best friends, and your colleagues all there to celebrate you. Imagine each one will stand to speak and share their story of *you*. They will share the stories of your work, your home life, your friendships, and your character. If they were to be truly honest, what would you want them to say about you? How would you want them to characterize you? How would you want them to describe your interactions? Your heart? What will they say about what motivates you? What drove you? How did you spend your time? What did your calendar look like? How did you spend your resources? How did you support them? How did you behave when times were challenging, and you were vulnerable?

While this is not an exhaustive list of potential questions, I now challenge you to sit down and write, or simply bullet point, what you want others to say about you when you retire. What do you want people to say about you? Take some time to define who you want to be and how you want to be known. After you have done so, you will find your why. When you know who you want to be, you will know your why. Because when you know who you aspire to be it reveals to you who you are and your motives. When you have uncovered your motives—that which drives you—it will shed light on the purpose of your life. Knowing your why will reveal your heart and give you guidance for your work. As you will reflect on what you have written, it will shine a light on the core of who you are and who you want to be. When you know your core, you will know your why, and when you know your why it will reveal to you who you are and give you fuel for how to become who you aspire to be.

A good friend of mine is a very successful independent insurance agent, and although to some this may seem like a relatively traditional way to make a living and support those she loves, she does this work not because she sells policies but because she loves caring for people. Not too long ago I simply asked about her work and why she got into this profession. As I asked this question, I could see her demeanor softened as if she positioned herself not to share with me her profit margin but share with me her heart. She explained it was not about selling insurance but it was about protecting people.

She explained that when people go through some of the most challenging times in their lives she is able to be a support post to help them stand and move through life. She explained how she had visited people who had undergone the loss of homes and their closest possessions, and she was able to provide a level of support to make their tragic circumstances a little easier. Yes, she sold insurance, but that wasn't her why. Her *why* was supporting and caring for people. Her *why* was being there for people during some of their most vulnerable times to help make the lives of others better. When she retires I imagine there will be a fleet of people who stand up and tell stories of her support, care, and love. Her *why* will be very clear.

Having meaning and purpose in our lives is at the core of our existence and loving ourselves means knowing ourselves and what we are purposed for. Again, take some time to write down what you would like others to say about you at your retirement party. Think about who you want to be and how you want to be remembered. When you have concretized this in writing, you will better know your purpose, and this will lead you to knowing how you want to position yourself in your work, with your spouse, with your children, and in your community. As your why comes into clearer focus, your motives will become more explicit, and your approach to life will shift. You may find that your interactions with people and work change and your perspective on all facets of life will grow deeper and lead to more wholeness. **Define yourself, know yourself, love yourself, and start filling your vessel with the *why* of your existence.**

Finding Purpose

Dr. Henry Cloud tells a story of two men who are both in the home-building business. In his story, he explains that the first builder described home building as a task to be completed and simply a way of making a living. This home builder felt that his work provided him with little meaning in his life. The first builder described that he basically takes a piece of land, builds a bunch of homes on it, makes a bunch of money, and then moves on to the next project. His view of the home building was transactional, it was devoid of significance and was nothing more than a vocation.

His work provided him with money and financial stability, but it did not provide him with purpose.

The second home builder Dr. Cloud described viewed his work very differently. This builder expressed joy and excitement in building homes. He shared the exhilaration he would get when helicoptering over the land envisioning the possibilities of a new community. The second builder, in his mind's eye, pictured what the community could offer to people's lives. He would imagine the stockings hung over the fireplace at Christmas time and children playing in the cul-de-sac. He could see a daughter walking down the stairs to meet her prom date and a family gathered in the kitchen to share a meal. The second builder in the story *chose* to find deep significance in his work. He saw home building as worthwhile and meaningful. Building homes brought families protection, security, and a place to create beautiful memories. For the second builder, building homes had purpose.

As leaders, if we are to value and care for ourselves we have to choose to find meaning in our work. When we do, there will be a greater sense of contentment in knowing that the way we spend our time is valuable. The story above illustrates that choice. Two home builders performing the same work. One makes a choice to see his work as empty, leaving him discontent. The other finds his work to be exhilarating and joyful because he can envision the impact it has on the lives of others. Two men, same job, each with a different perspective.

Research suggests that there are three ways of looking at our work. First, we can view our work as a way to simply make a living, pay the bills and provide for our needs and wants. Second, we can view our work as a means to elevate ourselves through achievement and social status. Finally, we can view our work as a *calling*, which provides us with a higher sense of purpose and is beneficial to our hearts.[8] Each of these choices has its consequences and if we choose to view our work and our leadership as a means of simply making a living or advancement, we miss the joy of finding the meaning in our work.

[8]Henry Cloud, *The Law of Happiness: How Ancient Wisdom and Modern Science Can Change Your Life* (New York: Simon and Schuster, 2011).

Several years ago, my uncle passed away. This was an uncle I didn't know very well growing up. He was distant and didn't really make an effort to be a part of our family. When he passed, there was no funeral, visitation, or services—just a written epitaph done by his second wife sent to the extended family and friends. It included most of his career highlights, his work, and his business accomplishments. There was no mention of a loving family, meaningful relationships, or his impact on the world other than that of his business dealings. It led me to ask: What was meaningful to him? What gave him purpose? How had his children viewed him? How would his children have described his life?

As leaders, we must know our purpose and how we are impacting the lives of those we lead and love. We have a choice to make as to how we view our lives and our work. If we expect to come to our seat of leadership fulfilled, we need to ensure that we are choosing to find value in the purpose of our leadership. Whether we are building buildings, teaching kids, managing grocery stores, selling coffee, or developing software we need to know that what we are doing is adding value to lives. From our seat of leadership, we are not just seeking our own accomplishments, we are seeking to bolster the lives of others. We are seeking to provide love and care for those we impact. In doing so, we have to know who we want to be and how we want to be remembered.

Much like our retirement speeches, we will be epitaphed. How will your children and spouse highlight your life? How will your children remember you? And what type of lessons will you have taught them about what is meaningful and valuable? When we have defined ourselves and we choose to see our leadership through a lens tinted in love we will find our vessels to be increasingly full and ready to pour into the lives of others. Loving yourself includes giving back to the world, finding your purpose, and creating your meaning. Research and love will both attest: when we give of ourselves, we will find ourselves, and we will find some of the greatest joy the human experience has to offer.

As we lead, let us be sure to recognize our vessel is full when we are leading with our whole selves for the purpose of making our homes, our offices, and our communities better.

Now *be* your retirement speech—to write it is not enough.

Summary

Our leadership journey starts with us. It starts with a deep understanding of ourselves and the motives that drive us. We need to know who we are at our core and who we intend to be for ourselves and others. Knowing our *why* and our purpose supports our living a more meaningful and impactful life through our leadership. When we have defined our purpose, we are better positioned to align our personhood to our work in a way that leads us to having a more purposeful and meaningful life. The love in leadership starts with us caring for our hearts and preparing our minds for leading others.

Love in Action

- How are you *choosing* to view your work? Do you view your work like the first or second home builder?
  - Sit with a peer, colleague, or friend and describe how your work serves others.
- What do you want others to say about you and how you have lived your life? How do you want to be remembered? What character qualities do you want to be remembered for?
  - Write a bulleted list of characteristics or qualities you would like people to say about you at your retirement party.
- What is your why? How does your purpose serve to better the lives of others? What is it that drives your work as a leader?
  - Write a journal entry describing and reflecting on what motivates you as a leader and why you lead others.

Chapter

Build Yourself by Building Others

If you get the inside right, the outside will fall into place.

—*Eckhart Tolle*

As leaders, we must cultivate an internal mindset that supports our own personal care and compassion. Caring for ourselves needs to be an integral part of our lives and adapting metacognitive processes that support self-care is vitally important to our work as leaders and those we lead. Metacognition is simply examining the way we think, looking *inward* at the way we frame situations in our minds, and dissecting the mindsets we adopt as we view the many facets of work and life. When we begin examining the way we think about our work as leaders, we have an opportunity to frame our efforts in a way that will lead to greater care for ourselves and add meaning to our work. Adopting a mindset in which we view our work in a service oriented and altruistic manner will allow us to find greater significance in our leadership.

Let's go back to the last chapter for just a moment, where we saw two home builders each taking opposing mindsets on essentially the same work. The builders had a choice in the way they viewed their work, much like you and I have a choice in the way we view our roles as leaders. Unfortunately, due to the nature of many leadership roles, we fall into negative mindsets because often our work is designed to solve problems, create solutions, identify the fault points, and the like. Oftentimes, by the very nature of our work, we create subconscious mental patterns that lead us to think more negatively about our work and the roles we play.

Let me share a lighthearted example to illustrate. A lawyer colleague of mine, with whom I have served on several negotiating teams, recently shared her experience with being what she jokingly referred to as the family chauffeur. She explained that when she is not dealing with late nights, hammering out union contracts, she is taking her two young children from soccer to dance, then to religious school and back to baseball. Every evening that she has free time she is trekking them all over the city. She expressed her total exhaustion. And while I am sure many parents can smile, empathize with, and understand this experience, I wanted to walk us through her mindset.

Although she may see this work as being tedious and uninteresting, and even though she jokingly expressed her evenings as being that of a glorified taxi driver, I know she does these tasks for a far more meaningful purpose. She does this to expose her children to fun and engaging learning activities. She desires to give her children greater opportunities in their lives; however, the way she negatively describes the experience as a chauffeur shines light on the way people often think. Her default mental script was to view the chauffeur experience as being negative despite the fact that what she is doing by driving her children to these experiences is deeply meaningful. Too often leaders, and people have default mental scripts that run in their minds that lead them to negative thinking about experiences. Being that leaders are positioned to solve problems, seek out areas of growth, and evaluate people and process over and over again, they have been conditioned to negative mental patterns that, when left unchecked, can lead to negative mindsets about work and leadership.

How many times have you worked with others, and they simply find the negative in any given situation? You could be in a meeting or just passing through the office and ask about the day, and they will shine light on the negative. You may say the weather is beautiful outside and they may complain that it is too hot or too humid. Hypothetically, you might share what a great job the presenter did, and they will agree and add, "But he could have been a little more ..." Whatever it is, our primal brains, in many ways, are wired for negativity to serve as protection. Our amygdales, the areas of our brain responsible for the Fight, Flight or Freeze response, will hijack our subconscious, and lead us to negative thinking—that is, our default unchecked human response is too often negative, and until we *metacognate* our way out of it we get stuck in negative pathways of thinking. As leaders who care deeply about ourselves and others, we have to take *responsibility*—that is, we have the *ability to respond*—for the way we think and the mental scripts that run through our minds. We have to think about the way we are thinking and choose to redefine our realities in a way that leads us to deeper meaning in our lives and our work. **We have to change the way we frame our experiences and choose a mindset with greater purpose and spirit.**

We can shift our mindsets by attaching prosocial behaviors to our leadership roles. Prosocial behaviors are simply those behaviors that benefit others such as sharing, cooperation, and volunteering. For example, when we give and serve others, we are presenting prosocial behaviors that, when performed, serve to give us a sense of personal fulfillment. We often perform prosocial behaviors because we feel a sense of responsibility to our fellow man and we have an altruistic sense to help support others.[9] When we frame our leadership roles in prosocial behavior, we direct our thinking to view our leadership as a form of service, giving back to others and performing altruistic service. Using metacognitive processes (thinking about how we are thinking) to control our perspective of our roles as leaders allows us to extract the value of what we do as leaders and in turn gives us a greater sense of altruism and purpose. Leading with an intentional mindset of service and giving allows us to give *ourselves* greater

---

[9]Dennis L. Poepsel and David A. Schroeder, "Helping and Prosocial Behavior." *HKU PSYC2020* 140 (2018).

love and value while in turn benefiting others. **Simply put, examine your thinking, adapt your mindset, and attach the prosocial value you offer as a leader.** One of the ways we can do that as leaders is to recognize that we lead to serve others.

Service

A friend of mine is the maintenance director of a midsize organization that includes six buildings. He is responsible for ensuring that each building is properly functional and that all systems are *go*! He is a mover and a shaker, there is no doubt, and he makes his rounds daily. He knows everyone's name in the organization and has close professional relationships with many. The amazing thing about my friend is he is dedicated to serving those in the organization. If there is a maintenance issue in any facility, he is happy to help, he is happy to serve. When he approaches a service call, his demeanor is positive, and his words are affirming. He understands the needs of his people and recognizes their dependence on his work. He cares about the people he helps every day, and he approaches his work with an almost Santa Clause–type jolliness, laughter, and humor. Although his role is maintenance, his true calling is service.

People who are content serve others. The beautiful thing about service is that it fills the cup of both the giver and the receiver. It's a gorgeous paradigm; when we give with giving hearts, it actually pays us back an even greater return. As leaders it is important for us to love ourselves through the act of service. Being able to provide support and give direction to those we lead serves not only to strengthen other individuals but it also serves to support our own moral core and social emotional foundations. One of the greatest things we can do in giving back is provide structures, routines, coaching and mentorship to our employees, children, and colleagues. Sergiovanni would contend that as leaders we have a moral obligation to serve and to empower those we lead.[10] **When our purpose for leadership is services and giving back, the perspective of our work and our lives will grow deeper and more meaningful.**

---

[10]Thomas J. Sergiovanni, *Moral Leadership: Getting to the Heart of School Improvement* (San Francisco: Jossey-Bass Inc., 1992).

Parenthetically, as we seek to give to others, it must be understood that servant leadership is not a form of weak leadership. This form of leadership does not enable poor performance or absolve others of their responsibilities to execute effectively. Let me illustrate. If as leaders we are serving others by providing them with clear and explicit expectations, and the employee does not achieve the desired outcome, it is *not* our role to perform their work. It is our role as leaders to support, coach, and teach that person, to the extent that their capacity allows, to execute their work. It is important for us to recognize that service to others is not the "I need to do this for them" form of leadership. To do so is not serving the best interest of that person or the organization. If that were the case, your service would be perpetuating the inability of that person to perform a task.

All of us, including the leader and those they lead, must *lift their own weights*. Let me explain. I use this analogy often with my daughter. It goes like this: If I were to take my daughter to the gym for the purpose of her to become healthier and stronger, I could *support* her by showing her how to use the machines and potentially create a workout plan for her to follow. I might teach her how to use weights machines that focus on targeted areas of the body. I may show her how to use the free weights and how to identify strain that is most appropriate for her. I would model and explain proper lifting techniques, how to avoid injury, and the importance of rest and stretching. Additionally, I might offer praise when she is performing the lifts appropriately and offer motivation if she struggles. This form of coaching and mentorship would be an appropriate form of *service*. Essentially, I would have given her the support she needed to be successful on her own and allow her to take ownership of her individual health and wellness goals.

On the contrary, I would be doing my daughter a great disservice if after we arrived I only modeled working out for her. If only *I* lifted the free weights and demonstrated the machines, she would not have an opportunity to feel the strain, to grow, or display her own new abilities. If, as the teacher, it was only myself who modeled the lifts, I would not have had an opportunity to offer her feedback, to praise her when she was hitting her mark, or encourage her when she struggled. By my lifting the weights for her, she would not grow stronger or learn how to manage her own workout routine. She would grow reliant on me to do it for her. In sum, I would have deprived her of the opportunity to lift her own weights, take ownership of her own health, and grow from her struggles. As leaders, we are not responsible for removing barriers to success and growth. We are responsible for serving and supporting in the form of coach, teacher, and mentor. In essence, *we need to let those we lead lift their own weights.*

As I mentioned above, servant leadership is not weak leadership. It does not enable or allow for poor performance. Servant leadership is about coaching, teaching, and support. It seeks to model and offer feedback in a way that builds capacity in people for their own personal and professional efficacy.

Coaching, Teaching, and Mentoring

I learned early in my life that there is a rejuvenating joy in being a teacher, mentor, and a coach. This form of service helps to fill our cups. When we serve others in these forms, it creates a sense of giving back, and there is an inherent personal benefit to that service. Let's remember that research supports that *giving people* are happier people and being a happier person leads to greater performance in all facets of our lives. In all areas of our lives, giving back as a coach, teacher, or mentor is a form of self-love. Parenthetically, let me mention that coaching and mentoring serve as an act of self-love and as an act of love toward others. I will touch upon both of these acts within this book. At this time, however, I will focus on the love of self in the mentoring relationship, and in part II I will focus on the love of others.

As I mentioned, it was early in my life when I discovered the love of service through teaching and coaching. As early as high school, I served as a peer counselor to underclassmen. In the program, we unpacked teen issues and discussed the real challenges students faced both socially and academically. I served students by offering guidance, experience and pointing them toward resources the school offered. The experience was exhilarating for me. Getting involved in real conversations and being able to help my peers was one of my first steps in being a coach, teacher, and mentor.

Today, after years of research, writing, and practicing the art of leadership coaching and mentoring, I can attest that it is equally as exhilarating. This form of service and giving back provides fire and energy to the soul, mind, and spirit. And while I will get deeper into the mentoring relationship later, the basic precepts of quality teaching, mentoring, and coaching include being intentional about your goals, fostering productive relationships, developing impactful structures and protocols, and being a living example.

Clear Goals

Tony Dungy, Super Bowl–winning NFL coach, expresses that the mentor leader is someone who focuses the mentoring relationship on developing specific strengths in the individual they are mentoring.[11] Ensuring that the purpose of coaching is specific and focused allows for greater effectiveness. Defining our goals and outcomes for our mentees allows for clear direction and a specific end game. Going back to the lifting weight analogy, the idea is not to lift the weights of others but to create a specific plan that will allow that individual to eventually lift their own weights, take ownership of their own performance, and add value to the organization and their own lives.

Productive Relationships

When we mentor, we have to recognize this as a form of service, and in doing so we are developing the foundation for the appropriate relational climate. As mentors, we are serving others and investing in their lives; therefore, serving our mentees with empathy, mindfulness, and compassion will allow for greater influence, impact, and learning. There is no shortcut to relationship building, and there is no one-size-fits-all approach; however, at their foundation, quality relationships rely on care, trust, and communication. Quality relationships depend on each of us being thoughtful and caring for one another. We must be people of integrity in order to build trust in both our personal and professional lives, and we must engage in regular communication that is meaningful, thoughtful, and focused. The basic fabric that binds us together as people is our ability to relate and build strong relationships with one another, and the mentoring relationship is no different.

---

[11]Tony Dungy, *The Mentor Leader: Secrets to Building People and Teams That Win Consistently* (Carol Stream, IL: Tyndale House Publishers, 2010).

Structure and Protocols

Teaching and mentoring require creating the right structures, systems, and protocols for our mentees. The development of structures and protocols is critical in all facets of our leadership, not to mention that of any coaching or teaching program. I cannot express enough—and I'll revisit this often throughout this book—that is the importance of developing specific systems and structures designed for intentional outcomes. For example, if we are coaching someone to become more physically healthy and to lose weight, we must be specific about their health and weight loss plan. A well-designed workout plan will include weight and cardiovascular training. Specific minutes of exercise will be prescribed, and the mentee will be held accountable by tracking their process and progress. Additionally, mentees will be placed on a specific diet and be required to track their calories, carbs, fats, and proteins. You get the drift. In order to achieve a specific outcome, our inputs have to be focused, prescriptive, and there must be structured accountability and tracking. This example is simple, but it is verified, and the precept is often missed in leadership. Too often people have unclear expectations, unclear measures, and expect specific outcomes. In order to achieve specific mentoring and teaching outcomes, there must be specific expectations and accountability measures.

Living Examples

We care for ourselves by giving back to others, and when we give back to others in the form of mentorship, coaching, or teaching we must be living examples. As leaders, our trust and integrity are paramount. We have to walk the walk and talk the talk. If we are seeking to create stronger organizations through developing others and building structurability, we have to demonstrate those same elements in our own lives. It is important that we model the appropriate mindset in our lives and in our work. The meaning and purpose of our work must be shared and exemplified, and we must develop routines and structures within our own lives that embody behaviors we are trying to teach. As leaders, our behaviors must typify what it means to be disciplined in thought and action. Our lives should represent what it is we stand for, who we want to be, and how we manage our lives in order to achieve results.

Service is one of the greatest virtues of the human experience. It is an awesome paradigm—in that, when we serve and invest in others, we fill a part of ourselves that longs for goodness and wholeness. There is a beauty in serving others that helps us to feel and understand our interconnectedness as human beings. Remember my maintenance friend I mentioned above? Each day his job is that of the maintenance director, but his calling is service to others. He chooses to see his work as deeply meaningful, and he provides a service to others that simply makes their lives better. **Seeing our leadership as a form of service is a choice that, when made, gives greater meaning and depth within our life experience.** When we choose a service mindset, we are indeed seeking to love ourselves by making our leadership journey more purposeful and relevant.

Giving

We make a living by what we get. We make a life by what we give.

—Winston Churchill

Leaders, in many respects, ask of others—that is, as parents, we ask our children to do the dishes; as bosses, we ask our employees to complete specific projects or meet certain goals. While this is perfectly reasonable, it must also be recognized that as leaders we are *givers* as well. Much like service is an act of virtue that fills our human spirits, giving also provides the same type of personal fulfillment that serves to make our lives more whole, complete, and connected to others. As leaders we must recognize that when we give it leads us to greater happiness and contentment and allows us to share our time, resourcefulness, and experiences with others.[12]

Early on in my career, I had the privilege of working with the second-largest school district in the state of Illinois. The district supported over forty thousand students and six thousand employees. During that time, one of the most impactful experiences I had was that of being connected to Nelvine, a top-performing principal who had developed a nationally recognized school and was consulting, teaching, and

---

[12]Anik, Lalin, et al. "Feeling good about giving: The benefits (and costs) of self-interested charitable behavior." *Harvard Business School Marketing Unit Working Paper*, 10–012 (2009).

mentoring others. Her experience and knowledge in building school culture and curriculum were exemplary and her desire to give back and share her experiences served to not only benefit me but also countless educational professionals around the country. She saw her work as an opportunity to give to others and to benefit thousands of administrators, teachers, and students. She framed her consulting and mentorship in a prosocial mindset, choosing to view her work as a form of generosity and big-heartedness, knowing that her work was benefiting others. She chose to give out of her experience, knowledge, time, and resources, which is, as leaders, what we have to offer those we are leading.

Giving Time

There are many forms of giving that range from giving gifts to random acts of kindness to time and effort. As leaders, one of the greatest ways we can give back is to offer our time to our employees, children, and those we lead and love. Offering focused, structured, and designed time to those we lead fosters their growth, development, and understanding. Leading means we set up regular and routine time to invest in others for their edification.

After leading many professional teams over the last twenty years, I can provide testimony to the benefit of regular and consistent time focused on the development of others. One specific team I worked with was a team of grade-level teacher leaders charged with the development of their grade-level curricula. These teacher leaders were responsible for directing the development of grade-level curriculum without having any positional authority within their grade-level team. Grade-level teacher leaders were essentially responsible for driving their teams forward without having any hierarchical position related to those they were leading. As one might suspect, this organizational structure created some challenges for those teacher leaders. Teacher leaders struggled with their roles as grade-level leaders, their knowledge of curriculum, and their comparative instructional knowledge related to those on their teams. Ensuring, however, that the grade-level teams were performing well together was critical to the success of this school district.

One of the essential components vital to the eventual success of the grade-level leaders was that of creating regular *time* to meet and lead their teams. Teacher leaders created weekly, monthly, and quarterly meeting times, allowing the teacher leaders and the teams to work through challenges, solve issues, and create consistent work patterns. The simple act of allocating *regular and focused* time allowed for the growth and success of these teams, and in this example I can testify that clear, focused, and consistent time given by the leaders resulted in the greater success of each and every grade-level team within that organization. **As leaders, we must recognize that offering and providing our time to others is a great benefit to others and we must frame that in our minds as a form of giving to others.**

Going back to Nelvine, she, too, offered specific and designed time to meet with myself and others for their edification. She did not have an open-door policy, but she did set aside time to share her experiences and her resources.

Intellectual Resources

A colleague of mine, Tim, owns and operates two medium-sized businesses related to commercial real estate and property management. He has a tenacious business sense and a drive and zest for his work and life that is contagious. On a weekly basis, he offers his time and his intellectual resources to his team and those who channel in remotely online. He offers weekly training sessions whereby he offers his intellectual resources to his team in an effort to support their growth and success. Mind you, their success is his success; however, he recognizes the importance of sharing specific business strategies and techniques that have led him to great success in the industry.

For Tim, sharing his intellectual resources is a valuable exercise that supports his desire to give back to others. In his weekly meetings, he shares business strategies that focus on improving the customer experience. He teaches on how to engage customers, improve customer satisfaction, increase customer loyalty, and develop return business. He also teaches about interpersonal skills and how to build strong and lasting professional relationships. He shares his strategies related to securing business contracts and growing further business opportunities. One of the great things about Tim's approach is his mindset. He chooses to see giving his intellectual resources as a form of altruism, not just business savvy. And while his approach is certainly smart business, he also recognizes that he is giving to those who will come after him, supporting their success and promoting their livelihood.

Sharing Experience

Offering our experience as leaders can serve as a meaningful form of giving to those we lead as well. In the world of hiring and retaining quality employees, *experience*, along with personal talent and education, is one of the great predictors of future success. Providing our experience is impactful, and sharing our examples, models, and knowledge will support the growth of our employees, students, and children.

In 2014, as part of an effort to train high-quality school principals and educational administrators, a large urban school district outside Chicago began developing an internal teacher to principal training program. Recognizing the shortage in quality principal candidates, the district decided to put forth effort in recruiting and training from within the organization. After many failed attempts to hire quality principal candidates from outside the organization, district leaders capitalized on internal candidates who had specific knowledge and experience within the organization. Internal candidates who had a working knowledge of the district's organizational structure and culture were able to navigate the organizational systems with greater ease, allowing for a more seamless transition from teacher to principal and ultimately administrative effectiveness.

The teacher to principal training program connected teachers to successful principals. Teachers and principals would meet regularly to perform specific training modules related to the principal performance standards. In so doing, acting principals would share their fruitful experiences and guide against pitfalls. Principals would walk their mentees through developing building level strategic plans, model leadership meetings, and work with teachers in understanding their role as classroom instructors. The program served to produce many successful principals, primarily through the sharing of experience. As we lead, maintaining a mindset in which sharing our experience is an act of giving and a form of prosocial behavior must become part of our metacognitive processes. **We must recognize that giving serves to fill our cups and is a foundational element in self-love.**

Summary

Susan David, author of *Emotional Agility*, reminds us that "we are the thinkers of our thoughts."[13] In other words, there is space between who we are and the thoughts we think. People are often unable to separate their thoughts from themselves. They choose not to metacognate, or think about their thinking and, in so doing, take on their thoughts as their own personal narrative. People fail to observe the subject—object relationship that exists with their thoughts and can be held hostage by their thoughts rather than stepping back from those thoughts, examining those thoughts, and choosing a response to those thoughts. In this chapter, I am asking you to think about your thoughts—metacognate. In that metacognition, more specifically, **I am asking you to think about your role as a leader, a parent, or within your local community and choose to attach the prosocial behaviors of giving and service to your emotional identity as a form of self-love and self-care.**

Leading from a place of altruism and accepting your role as a servant leader, contributing to others, supports your emotional well-being. The choice is yours. How you choose to view your thoughts about your leadership role is vital to defining yourself as a leader. Choosing to be a leader who is purposed for service, promoting the well-being of others, requires intentional thinking. Within that intentional thinking, you will find that serving and giving to others is at the core of our humanity, and in that mind frame you find greater purpose, meaning, and love in your own life.

Love in Action

- How do you frame your leadership role? Is your leadership an altruistic endeavor?

---

[13]Susan David, *Emotional Agility: Get Unstuck, Embrace Change, and Thrive in Work and Life* (New York: Penguin Press, 2016).

- o In your next team meeting, have you and your teammates share your leadership journey. Ask: What brings you to this point in your career, and how does your role serve others?

- Is there an opportunity to attach prosocial behaviors to your work? Are you giving? How do you serve those you lead?

  - o Take a moment and list the prosocial behaviors that you attach to your work and your actions as a leader.

- How do you share your time, intellectual resources, and experience?

  - o Put on your calendar intentional time to share your time and resources with those you lead. Small ten-to-fifteen-minute conversations can serve to support and build those we lead.

Chapter

Designing Yourself through Positive Habits

We first make our habits, and then our habits make us.

—John Dryden

While we have seen that loving and caring for ourselves comes in the context of understanding our purpose and creating a personal mindset of service and giving, we must also include developing and sustaining positive habits in our lives. In a recent lecture I attended, the presenter asked the crowd, "How many of you believe that people are motivated 100 percent of the time?" Just a few hands were raised in the audience. People did not feel as if themselves, or others, were motivated 100 percent of the time. The presenter proceeded to tell us how we were wrong. He explained that we *are* motivated 100 percent, and because we are, our actions reflect our motivations 100 percent of the time. Let me explain.

In asking the question, the presenter was seeking to point out to us that we are always motivated. That motivation may not be in line with our intentions or our values, but we are motivated, and we do act according to our motivations. For example, many high achievers report they have a habit of reading at least thirty minutes per day. Reading provides them with new ideas, increased intellect and stimulates thinking. Many would probably agree that this would be a valuable exercise, one worth incorporating into their daily routine. In order to make reading thirty minutes per day a habit, individuals must create that time in their daily routines or calendars. In doing so, some may decide in order to create this habit they will get up thirty minutes earlier each morning to start reading.

Let us imagine that on day one of performing this new habit we may be highly motivated to get out of bed and start our new self-improvement habit. We are jazzed up to get our new habit underway, and our level of enthusiasm has peaked. After a few days of incorporating this habit into our daily routine, however, we start to feel less enthused. We start wanting to sleep later. We hit the snooze button and allow ourselves a few extra minutes to enjoy our restful bliss, and after a few more days our thirty-minute reading habit has been put on the shelf. Why? Because we were not motivated? No, we were motivated. We were just motivated to sleep in. We had a choice. Sleep in or get up and read. We like the idea of getting up and reading. It aligns with our values. But we were *motivated* to stay in bed. We value reading thirty minutes every morning, but when that value conflicts with our value of sleep, out motivation for sleep won out.

We are motivated 100 percent of the time, either to sleep, read, exercise, meditate, journal, and the list goes one. It is critically important as leaders that we understand how to develop the habits of self-love that will allow us to be our best selves in order to further our purpose and support those we lead. Charles Duhigg, in his book *The Power of Habits*, explains what he refers to as the habit loop.[14] The brain, Duhigg explains, is constantly looking to spend less energy making decisions and is therefore seeking to develop habits and routines to systemize our daily lives. How many times have you

---

[14]Charles Duhigg, *The Power of Habit: Why We Do What We Do in Life and Business* (New York: Random House, 2012).

driven to work and realize you're halfway there and you can barely remember the drive? You have essentially operated on auto pilot for miles because your brain has developed the neuro pathways to lead you to work without your conscious awareness having to spend energy. Your brain developed a habit that requires it to spend less energy navigating and making decisions.

While your brain is seeking ways to systemize and organize your life, it has created some very habitual routines and ways of thinking. The habit loop Duhigg describes is the catalyst for the development of these habits. Our habits are formed out of a simple loop, which includes a trigger or cue, a routine, and a reward for that routine. Triggers can be intellectual, physical, or emotional and lead to a routine that is worth engagement. One small but powerful example I have developed in my life stemmed from my connection to my church and my faith. I refer to this habit as my "morning chair" routine. I have had this habit for over ten years, and it started as a challenge presented by the leaders of my church. Our senior pastor challenged us to read our Bibles for fifteen minutes a day and think about how we responded spiritually. Being spiritually and intellectually motivated, I immediately took on this challenge, and I found quickly that this routine did provide a reward. I found that my mornings were more spiritually focused, and my day started with a spiritual perspective that I personally longed for.

Starting this new habit, like starting any new habit, did take effort and inertia to get it off the ground. I had set aside some time in my morning routine for my morning chair time. Initially, like many of us starting new habits, I went through what Jason Selk refers to as the honeymoon phase[15]—that is, I was excited to start my new habit, and my motivation was high. We see similar honeymoon phases in dating, relationships, and other new experiences as well. After a few days, or even weeks, the honeymoon fades as we find ourselves struggling to maintain our new habit. Selk refers to this as the fight through period, in which we must fight through this temporary lack of motivation to maintain this habit.

---

[15]Jason Selk, "Habit Formation: The 21-Day Myth," *Forbes*, 2013.

One way we can fight through to maintain habits is through a practice called life projection. In *life projecting*, we imagine ourselves in the future looking backward and thanking ourselves for having developed this habit. Or we imagine how we would feel looking backward if we did not continue with this habit. Life projecting allows us to inject a little mental motivation to help us push through after that honeymoon phase has come to an end. In my personal example, the honeymoon phase came to an end after several days. I reverted back to my old pattern of sleeping in just a little later. But I did eventually push through because I connected more deeply to the reward, which eventually served as my trigger. After missing my morning chair for a few days, I realized how much I did appreciate the beauty of that spiritual time in my life, and life projecting allowed me to see how much I was missing from forgoing that time for just a few extra minutes of sleep.

Working through habit development is not always easy, and certainly some habits are harder to maintain and develop or even break than others. But leaders must fight through to develop and maintain positive habits in their lives to be able to be highly effective players in the arena.

Mindfulness

One of the most impactful ways to care for ourselves is through the development of mindful habits and practices. Mindfulness injects us with a keen awareness of our body, mind, heart, and spirit.[16] It promotes a deep sense of openness and oneness within ourselves, and it allows us to step away from yourself and experience our lives through a clear mental consciousness. It enables us to slow our thinking, be highly metacognitive, and be in the moment to examine our thoughts and emotions. Developing mindful habits leads to a higher level of wisdom, self-awareness, and spirituality that will indeed impact your life as a person and as a leader. Mountains of research support the benefits of mindfulness and there are many ways to practice mindfulness, but in order to do so we must be intentional about developing mindful habits.

---

[16]Annie McKee and Richard E. Boyatzis, *Resonant Leadership: Renewing Yourself and Connecting with Others through Mindfulness, Hope, and Compassion* (Boston: Harvard Business Press, 2005).

In order to practice mindfulness and reap its rewards, we must set aside time to do so. Establishing consistent mindful routines and habits allows us to carry our best selves into the workplace and our homes. Carving time out of our daily lives and ensuring that mindful practices make their way on to our calendar is the first step in ensuring that self-awareness becomes part of our daily lives. One way that I have ensured that I practice mindfulness is through my *morning chair* that I mentioned above. It is thirty minutes I set aside each morning in which I infuse reading, prayer, and mediation into my life, allowing me to have greater mental focus, slow my thinking, and examine underlying emotions or thoughts I am feeling.

My morning chair is just the way that I choose to reach a mindful state. Another way we can infuse mindfulness is through meditation. Mediation involves allowing yourself an opportunity to release your thoughts and get in close connection with the purest form of your consciousness. Let's do a little exercise for just a moment. Close your eyes and take ten slow deep breaths without thinking any thoughts. That's right—simply close your eyes and just concentrate on taking ten deep breaths, in and out, simply focusing on your breathing. Go ahead—I'll wait.

How'd it go? For many of us, this can actually be quite difficult. As we begin breathing, simple thoughts start to creep into our minds. We start thinking about our lives or our list of to-dos. We start asking ourselves questions like: Did we come across the right way in that meeting? Did I say the right thing to my daughter? Do I need to cut the grass, or can I wait until tomorrow? It's as if our minds, our psyches, have a mind of their own. Our minds and our thoughts just seem to run full throttle without us even touching the gas! It is true, our psyche is constantly working to navigate the world, solve problems and make life manageable for us all while running in the background without much intentionally focused effort on our part.

Meditation is the process by which we delineate the thinker from the thought. Mediation is where we recognize that we are not our thoughts, and we take deliberate steps to get intimately close to the thinker (our consciousness) while setting aside our thoughts. There are many ways to do this, and like all habits, it takes practice.

One way to reach a meditative state is to do exactly what I mentioned above. Take a few moments to get into a comfortable posture and take in deep breaths allowing yourself to exhale slowly. As you take in each breath, feel the oxygen enter and exit your body and imagine the air filling your body. Imagine that breath filling your entire body all the way from your chest through your legs and arms to your toes and fingers. Practice this. Allow yourself to focus only on your breathing and your physical state, while setting aside any other thoughts. When other thoughts start to creep in, recognize them simply as thoughts, set them aside as if passing by them on the highway, and refocus on your breathing. Relax into your breathing. Let go of your thoughts and feel your awareness. Get close to the clearest sense of consciousness that you can, and allow yourself to be your truest form, free from thoughts and emotions.

Meditative breathing is just one way to infuse mindfulness into your life. If you value mindful meditation practices and find that sitting is not your preferred method, you might also want to try mindful walking. Much like mindful breathing, mindful walking requires you to be clearly focused on your body and its movements while relinquishing your other thoughts. While engaging in mindful walking, you may choose to concentrate on each step you take, focusing on the way each heel touches the ground and the roll of your feet. You may want to focus on the swing of your arms or the slight rotation of your shoulders. You may also prefer to concentrate on the way your whole body is moving through time and space, getting a deep sense of your physical being and your position in the universe. If you are able to be in nature, you may want to take a moment to realize the symbiotic qualities you share with nature. You may want to take in the sunlight or feel your being in the larger picture of nature, swimming in an ocean of air that sinks deeply into your lungs and then departs. Whatever your choice or however you choose to mindfully walk, use it as an opportunity to love your body and mind and get close to your simple consciousness.

Another mindful practice I learned in the fifth grade from my teacher, Mr. Wallace, is called the body scan. Now in my forties, I still practice this. Body scan requires you to take a comfortable posture, preferably lying down. While lying down you focus on the sensation of each part of your body. Typically, you might start by imagining you are in one of your most desirable places, floating on a cloud or sitting on a beach, and you begin by feeling the sensation of your toes. From your toes you move upward through your ankles, lower legs, upper legs, through to your pelvis, lower back, upper back, and stomach. You may scan your fingers tips up through your arms to your shoulders. Then you may finish by releasing the tensions in your head and neck. Body scan is simply another way to put yourself into a mindful and meditative state allowing yourself to relax, control, and release your thoughts.

Mediation is a practice that takes time to develop, so give yourself some time and grace in improving. Over time, after you have developed this habit, you will experience the many benefits mindfulness and mediation have to offer. You will start to be able to calm yourself and manage your thoughts. You will start to be able to separate the thinker from the thought and be able to navigate your thoughts and feelings more clearly with greater metacognition and perspective. Meditation will allow you to see your thoughts for simply what they are, thoughts, and allow you to answer them with a measured and metered response. It will also allow you to let unworthy thoughts, feelings and emotions pass by as if you were simply driving past them in your car. You will recognize them, see them, look at them from inside the car and just simply allow them to fade in your rearview mirror. Meditation is a beautiful and powerful habit and can be performed in many ways, my examples are certainly not the only ways, and you should feel compelled to search out what works best for you.

Yoga

Another mindful practice is yoga. Yoga not only treats the mind but it also treats the spirit and body. Remember, as leaders it is critical that we are caring and loving of ourselves. Ensuring that our mind, body, and spirit are cared for is our responsibility, and yoga is a very effective mindful practice. Much like meditation, yoga seeks to draw our minds to a quiet place of self-awareness. Yoga practices lead us to being more in tune with ourselves, our bodies, our minds, and our emotions. Drawing on ancient practices, yoga promotes being at peace with ourselves, our families, and our communities. It tends to our physical bodies by walking us through a series of movements that lead to increased flexibility, stamina, and strength. The techniques prescribed through yoga practices are beneficial to the mind, soul, and nervous system. And while you may not want to run out and join your local yoga studio, there are many online tutorials that can lead to a very beneficial and mindful yoga experience. YouTube is a great place to start.

Journaling

Parenting can and is a beautiful and a challenging experience. It forces us to think about life in a very purposeful and intentional way. As parents, we try and support, coach, love and lead our children to better lives. We attempt to provide them with all the great experiences that lead them to becoming intelligent, mindful, caring, successful people. I remember most recently, when my child was selecting a college, how much I wanted to impact her decision-making. We had visited what I believed to be a really awesome school down in the southeast, and I thought for sure this would make for an awesome place for dads' weekend (great college football to be had here) and to offer her a great college experience. I could see her trekking around the beautiful brick campus on her bike, loving her journey and soaking up every opportunity. In my mind this was it, this was the place to start her college career.

And while I share all that with you, I tried not to project my wishes on her. As much as I was really excited about her attending school at this university, I tried not to allow my enthusiasm for this school to influence her decision. As we went through the college selection process, I had to be very deliberate about unpacking my thoughts and understanding my thoughts related to my child selecting a school. And in keeping my thoughts contained and understood, I journaled the experience, solidifying my thoughts in writing allowed me to both metacognate and to be introspective. Journaling supports the examination of our thinking and our experiences by capturing them in writing and being able to literally look at and read them back to ourselves. Journaling forces us to recreate our thoughts, feelings, actions, on paper (or computer screen, if you prefer) and get behind those thoughts. As I mentioned above, we are the *thinkers*—that is, we are the subject. Our thoughts are things; they are objects we view through our conscious lens. Journaling sets the stage for the thinker to write the thoughts, therefore, separating the thought from the thinker and providing the thinker with greater perspective on those thoughts. The thinker can unpack those thoughts, validate those thoughts, and determine if those thoughts are worthwhile, true, and beneficial. When we, as subject, as thinker, are able to lay our thoughts before us it gives us greater perspective and provides us with time to inspect our thoughts and feelings. Simply taking the time to journal furthers our ability to respond in an intentional and thoughtful manner.

As I worked through the college selection process and captured my thoughts in my journal, it allowed me to see that I *was* projecting my desires and preferences on to my daughter. My thoughts and feelings were *my* preferences about what type of school she should want to attend and what type of excitement the football team should produce—after all, what is college these days if you can't rave about the football team! All joking aside, I was projecting. I was projecting my thoughts, beliefs, and preferences about college onto my daughter. I was very careful, however, not to share that with her in a way that would persuade her too much! As the college visitation continued, and it was time to make a selection, we discussed the pros and cons of each school, and I believe she chose the best school for her and for her personality, academic desires, and with the best internship possibilities. I have been proud of her thoughtfulness throughout the decision-making process, and I am also glad I was able to slow my thinking, examine my thoughts, put them down on paper, and determine my ability to respond.

While journaling is a powerful tool and a habit that is worth cultivating, it doesn't have to just be about specific experiences. You can explore journaling in many positive ways, which will undoubtedly create a fuller, more spirited you. Briefly, some other ways that people prefer to journal is through prayer—that is, many people take the time to write down their prayers to their God, which, by engaging the senses through the physical act of writing, solidifies prayer and can make it deeper and more meaningful. Others chose to create a gratitude journal. Reflecting on what we are thankful for leads to increased happiness and contentment.[17] Still further, others chose to keep a positive reflection journal capturing the beauty that takes place in all the little and small ways. Individuals will simply write down a few of the beautiful moments that have taken place in their lives and reflect upon those moments. Journaling is powerful. It can take many forms, it creates meaning, and it allows us to reflect and examine the beauty of our lives. It allows us to love ourselves through a very intentional act. If this is something that inspires action, I recommend doing more research on the topic for your benefit. I promise daily writing has a lot to offer!

Supporting Our Bodies

A few years back, I had a close colleague whom I worked with that underwent a complete and total body transformation. I am so happy to be able to share this because seeing someone go from a place of unhappiness, unhealthiness, and obesity to a person whose smile is infectious and who is confident and happy is a joyful experience. At the time I met her, my colleague was working through her doctorate program and had two teenage boys who were very into athletics. She mentioned she was taking these boys to their practices every night and that she also served as their leader of the fundraising committee. She was also a vice president in her organization and had a lot of professional responsibilities that demanded her attention. On top of her work at home, and within her profession, she was writing her dissertation, which is no small feat. She was burning the candle at both ends and she knew it. She was obese, unhealthy, and taking very little time to love herself or her body. She knew she needed to change, or she wasn't going to be around to see her boys get married or hold her grandkids one day. And with all the willpower and effort she could muster she started to make simple, small, habitual changes that produced great rewards.

She started by planning and managing the way she ate. She simply spent a few hours each week preparing her meals for the entire week. By planning and being thoughtful about her meals, she was able to

---

[17]Henry Cloud, *The Law of Happiness: How Ancient Wisdom and Modern Science Can Change Your Life* (New York: Simon and Schuster, 2011).

manage what she was eating and her caloric intake. And while some may find excuses in the time it takes to prepare meals, she explained how she got hours of her life back each week. She described how she would spend a few hours each weekend planning and preparing what she planned to eat for the entire week. She explained that by spending two to three hours planning on one day it saved her the individual daily tasks of deciding what to eat and how to prepare. Rather than spending energy each day and at every meal determining what she was going to eat, how it was to be prepared, she changed her routine and spent just a few hours on Sunday managing all those choices for the week.

When she was living an unhealthy lifestyle she was spending time each day deciding what she wanted to eat and when she didn't have the willpower to cook or prepare a healthy meal, she would often default to food that was quick, easy, and unhealthy. Through the small act of developing a weekly meal preparation plan she developed healthy habits through the triggers, routine, and reward loop. The reward was not just feeling confident, being healthier, and looking great but it was also getting hours back in her life by making her weekly eating habits easier, more routine, and efficient. She was saving time, solidifying healthy eating habits, and not exhausting herself through daily decision-making. Weekly meal preparation served to make her life healthier, simpler, happier, and easier. The results of her self-love were beautiful.

In addition to her meal preparation routine, she was also careful about her workout and exercise routine. She made strong gains in feeling great about herself and her health through a combination of intentional dietary preparation and physical activity. Her exercise routine was specifically based upon her age, her specific goals, and her abilities; however, the basic premise that physical activity is good for the body and spirit remains true for all of us. When deciding on a workout plan, it is important to take into consideration your current condition, age, and goals. It would serve you to see a doctor, dietician, and workout professional to assist you along your journey. Experiencing the benefits of exercise can be exciting, fun, and invigorating. Activities like hiking, biking, and swimming are not only beneficial for strength and wellness but they can also be a lot of fun! Yoga, as mentioned above, is not only beneficial physically but also allows us to strengthen our mindfulness muscles. Cycling classes and other group fitness classes can be a blast as well. Finding workout friends can add personal connections and accountability to your healthy lifestyle. Racquetball, volleyball, soccer, and the like are also great ways to make exercise fun and recreational. There are so many ways to make working out a part of your healthy lifestyle. Making exercise enjoyable and offering yourself some variety in your workouts can serve to help keep you motivated and driven along your self-care voyage. Remember your future self? What will he or she thank you for in the future that you can do today? Take some time to plan your meals and develop a workout routine. Care and love yourself through the intentional act of eating healthy and exercise.

As leaders, if we want to lead people to being their best and most productive selves, we have to model healthy living every day. Exemplifying self-discipline in our thoughts and actions is critical in our being impactful leaders. When we can embody what it means to lead healthy, productive, and disciplined lives, we are able to share the fulfillment that comes with those healthy and fulfilling habits. A caveat here: When I say *share*, I do not mean pushing your habits on people in a negative way—that is, I don't mean being arrogant or being a know-it-all, telling everyone how disciplined you are while they may not be. I mean being a living example that is humble and hungry to create a contagiously beautiful life. I mean sharing yourself as an example in terms of action, not overly sharing with words. With that said, let's enjoy the small wins each day that we make healthy choices and let us enjoy the rewards.

Acts of Kindness

Leadership, in any arena, can undoubtedly be taxing, and over long periods of time it can wear on our minds and hearts. We can doubt ourselves, fear our abilities, and question our effectiveness, to say the least. In leadership there are many situations that can push stress and anxiety our way, which is why it is so vitally important to care for ourselves in the ways I have described above. In addition to taking the time to develop positive habits and a healthy and self-loving lifestyle, there are the very intentional acts of kindness that will serve to create little bursts of hope, positivity, and perspective in our lives.

I have a good friend who runs a small salon. In his business, he cuts mostly men's hair and does a good job of maintaining a solid client base. He is probably one of the more unique people I have met. He is very genuine and slightly eccentric. He reminds me of an eighties hair-band rock star. He is not religious, and I am not sure if he is even spiritual; however, he serves at a local church providing haircuts to the homeless. He has shared a few stories with me about how people feel after getting a haircut. He explained that people feel valued and respected after they get cleaned up. They feel more accepted in public when they are looking clean and feeling confident. I share this story because I think it is beautiful and kind. My friend takes time to care for people. He uses his time to share his gifts and talents in very simple and tangible ways. And although he makes no money cutting the hair of the homeless, his acts of kindness pay huge dividends in his heart and mind. The joy and spiritedness he feels are strong, and I know there is a wonderful reward he gets from serving and volunteering in this way. In his giving to others, he is indeed creating beauty and love within himself. It is again that awesome paradigm that when we give to others we are actually receiving deep in our hearts and souls.

Acts of kindness can be expressed in so many ways and can be fun and spontaneous. Simple ways that leaders can spread a little kindness is through handwritten notes. Spending just a few moments to write a note of thanks or positivity to a colleague, family member, or friend can serve to inspire the hearts and minds of both the giver and receiver.

When driving along the tollway, sometimes people will choose to pay the toll for the person behind them. This always surprises the receiver and encourages others to pay it forward. In other ways, people will donate food, clothing, or other goods. Welcoming people as they come into the office, school, or church is also a spirited act of kindness. Undoubtedly, there are endless ways we can express small and simple acts of kindness that will truly serve to strengthen our hearts, minds, and purpose. Now we know that random act of kindness fuels our spirit, but it is important to actually do them—that is, like any habit, we must be intentional about the trigger, the routines, and the rewards that allow us to develop, strengthen, and maintain our habits.

Gratitudes

One of the quotes that has left deep tire tracks in my brain and on my heart is a quote by Henry Allen Ironside, which reads: "We would worry less if we praised more. Thanksgiving is the enemy of discontent and dissatisfaction." I lean on this quote often if I find myself in a state of worry or discontent. As leaders, we will often find ourselves in situations of stress and anxiety. Stress will undoubtedly abound as we seek to move forward in our homes and in our businesses. It is important that we recognize the value of slowing down and being mindful of our blessings, which paradoxically leads to a more content mental state.

As we approach self-care and self-love, we must remember these are habits we have control over that lead to a greater sense of peace, contentment, and fullness. We have to understand that there are both things within our control and things outside our control. Ancient stoic philosopher Epictetus spoke about the ability of people to recognize the things that were within their control and those things that were not. He focused heavily on teaching his students about the things within their control. He posits that we can control our thoughts, habits, and our responses to the world. When we are able to do so, we can live a happier and more fulfilled life. I find it profound that after nearly two thousand years since Epictetus's passing, we are still challenged in recognizing that *we do have some control* over our thoughts, emotions, and habits. While there are so many things, such as age, natural hair color, and death, that are out of our control, we do have the opportunity to recognize our thoughts and manage our habits. In doing so, we have the opportunity to manage our contentment by taking inventory of the many blessings we have.

Much like the habits of meditation, exercise, and journaling, gratitude is a habit that when cultivated can produce deep fulfillment. We can express our gratitude in many ways. Some may choose to combine habits and choose a gratitude journal. Others may choose to express gratitude through daily prayer. Others may choose to share gratitude through notes of thanks to others or just sharing during the breaking of bread. The point here is this; we must be intentional about our gratitude. Taking inventory of our gifts, blessings, and our mental state will allow us to create mental impressions in our psyche that focus on positive experiences. And as we train our brains through gratitude exercises, we will build up mental muscle to view our world through a lens of thankfulness and praise rather than discontent.

Further, praise and gratitude should also be expressed in times of struggle and growth. In James chapter 1 of the Bible, he expresses that we should "Consider it pure joy, my brothers and sisters, whenever you face trials of many kinds, because you know that the testing of your faith produces perseverance."[18] Here James reminds us that our struggles should and can produce joy and perseverance. In other words, we should be thankful for our struggles, challenges, and trials because they will make us stronger and more complete individuals. Unfortunately, many of us have come to believe that struggle, challenge, and stress are inherently negative experiences. I would argue that when appropriately framed in our psyche, struggle and stress can lead to great growth, focus and determination.

For example, let's talk about having to meet deadlines as a cause of stress. Ask any college student how they feel about meeting end of semester deadlines, and they will share with you their stress. While they are in the midst of completing final projects or preparing for finals, their stress may seem quite burdensome. Now, ask that same college student how they feel after the semester has ended and you will often get a sense of their resolve and their thankfulness. Thankfulness because their hard work produced positive results and achievements.

Thankfulness does not need to be set aside for exclusively positive experiences but should also be expressed through our trials and struggles because we know that these experiences, if framed correctly, will sharpen our focus, build our mental muscle, and lead

---

[18]Bible. NIV. James 1:2–3.

us to higher ground. Challenges, trials, and struggles have the potential to lead to thankfulness if we choose to find the lessons within them. Being grateful for challenges and struggles can bring us joy, feed our spirits, and fill our cups. Cultivating habits of gratitude is our individual responsibility, and when we do, we'll be building mental muscle leading to a more meaningful and fulfilling life.

Summary

At this point, you might be thinking these habits are seemingly common sense. With the recent research coming from the world of positive psychology touting the routines of happiness, contentment, and fulfillment these habits are ubiquitous in current literature. I would argue, however, that while common sense may certainly be common, common actions are undoubtedly not. Knowing and doing are two very different practices and although people may be very well aware of the habits, rituals, and routines that would lead to greater fulfillment in their lives, they too often lack the ability to leverage their motivations to develop such habits.

Being able to manage and infuse knowledge and positive routines into our lives has been a challenge for many and the statistics related obesity in America are a testimony to people's inability to manage their lives in a positive manner. The Centers for Disease Control shared most recently that over 42 percent of adults between forty and fifty-nine are obese.[19] Despite the mountains of evidence that validates that obesity leads to cancer, diabetes, heart disease and a multitude of other health maladies over 42 percent of people in the United States continue poor diet and exercise habits. If we want to be better leaders and examples for those in our care, we must take the time to develop positive habits that lead to our own personal care, love, and fulfillment. (Please know I recognize that not all obesity is related to controllable circumstances, nor do I intend to offend)

The habits of mindfulness, yoga, journaling, meditation, gratitude, kindness, and exercise are undoubtedly positive habits that will lead to a life of greater meaning, fulfillment, and achievement; however, knowing them is the easy part. Putting them into practice requires

---

[19]https://www.cdc.gov/obesity/data/adult.html.

effort and energy. As I mentioned above, habits are developed through the habit loop of trigger, routine, and reward. Developing those triggers in your life and designing your mindset to capture the benefits of your habits is critical in getting started. In addition to setting and designing your triggers, I also mentioned the importance of life projecting. Sometimes when we are unmotivated we need to get in touch with our future selves. We need to frame our thinking and reward our future selves with our actions today. Viktor Frankl, author of the *Man's Search for Meaning*, puts it this way—"Live as if you were living for the second time around."

Beyond sparking our triggers and rewarding our future selves we need to start small and develop small wins. This is critical to habit development. Fitness companies make a fortune on people who start new gym memberships at the beginning of the year and fail to show up after three weeks. Why? Because people fail to see the importance of small wins. People will often sign up and start their new exercise routine with as much gusto as they can muster. They put forth a tremendous amount of mental positive energy in starting their exercise routine. After a day or two, they find themselves very sore and hurting after a few challenging workouts. After the first week or so, the thought of going back is equated to the pain of the gym rather than the reward. When those hard workouts don't produce instant results, people soon fall off and return to their more sedentary lifestyles.

If, however, new habits are started small, very different results may be found. If individuals started with smaller, less challenging workouts, they would not leave the gym exhausted and in pain, and overtime the simple habit of going to the gym would develop. The reward of simply going to the gym would begin to grow roots in their minds and the development of the habit would solidify. Over time the trigger would become the reward of going to the gym and the grounded habit would open the door for more challenging and impactful workouts. The same should be said of all the habits mentioned above. Starting small is impactful in developing sustained habits and we should allow ourselves some room to grow and succeed. Rushing full bore into a new habit may lead to over exertion and burnout, therefore, as you develop your new habits give yourself some grace to start small and celebrate small wins.

In addition to starting small, we must also not allow perfection to be our enemy. Too often, when starting new habits, we find ourselves stumbling. It is a challenge to start new habits and routines, and getting them off the ground undoubtedly takes strength and effort. As mentioned, it takes focus and mental energy to see our future selves and frame our thoughts and emotions. Giving ourselves grace and understanding lets us appreciate that we will stumble. Let us recognize that developing new habits is hard and allow ourselves to simply fail, then pick up where we left off and continue our efforts.

Most recently, a media campaign designed to discourage people from smoking was launched. It expressed that people who eventually quit smoking had attempted to do so several times before actually kicking the habit for good. Contrary to the failed "Just Say No" antidrug campaign of the 1980s, which grossly oversimplified the issue of habit development, this antismoking campaign takes into account the difficulty of developing or ceasing a habit. In the campaign, there are testimonials by people who have stopped smoking and their failed attempts before doing so. One of the testimonials includes a woman sharing how at one time she had stopped by constantly keeping her hands busy. But a few weeks of keeping her hands busy was just not enough, and she eventually returned to smoking. She goes on to share that it took her seven failed attempts to stop smoking before she was finally successful. Now, had she simply given up after her first or even fifth attempt she would not have been able to cease the habit of smoking. Had she allowed perfection to be her enemy she would still be smoking today. For those of us looking to sustain new habits that will breathe life into our hearts and minds, we must recognize that we will fail. Our path to new habit development will not be perfect and we will fall short at times. The key, however, is to continue right where you left off. If you have failed to exercise for a few a week, let it go, and start small again. If you are missing your morning meditations, don't beat yourself up about it. Move forward tomorrow. New habits will not develop without their struggles. Embrace those challenges, start small, see your future self, and hold on to knowing you are growing and making your life better just a little bit at a time.

As leaders in any arena, caring for ourselves, loving ourselves, and creating more meaningful, passionate, and impactful lives takes effort. It takes the intentional infusion of life-giving habits into our lives. I challenge us to care for ourselves and love ourselves so that we can step into our homes, offices, and community settings with the strength and the personal integrity to make the lives of others better around us.

Love in Action

- What would your future self thank you for doing today? What habits would your future self want you to develop today?
    - List one or two areas that you would want to focus on for self-improvement. Keep it simple and start small.
- What rewards can you capture in your mind that will trigger your sustaining a new positive habit?
    - After identifying a new habit that you would like to focus on, create a list of small rewards that would entice you to maintain this habit.
- Where might you struggle with a new habit and how can you relinquish perfection in order to start again?
    - Take action to remind yourself that you will fail, but to keep going. Where can you keep your mantra to persevere so that you see it every day you are developing this new habit.
- Are you allowing time for positive habits in your life, such as journaling, mindfulness, yoga, prayer, exercise, meal preparation, gratitude, kindness, etc.?
    - Take an inventory of your positive habits. Take some time to think or write about your current reality. List what you are already doing. Get a clear picture of what you are currently working on, how it is working, and what you can do to build upon that positive experience. From that point, decide to strengthen those positive habits or use the same habit-building strategy to a build new one.

Chapter

Intentional Well-Being

Between stimulus and response there is a space. In that space is our power to choose our response. In our response lies our growth and our freedom.

—Viktor Frankl

Let me offer a brief summary up to this point. Recently, I was conducting a weeklong professional growth summit for my teaching staff. It has become a common practice in which I seek the input from those on the front lines of the organization and put together a lineup of experts in our field to share best practices. One of the experts I have drawn from the last several years began her presentation by asking, "Why are you important?" Each teacher in the audience was asked to respond to the whole group. As we went around the room, it was eye-opening to hear people struggle with their answers. It was as if they were caught off guard. As if they hadn't thought about their contributions to their students or their community. Like many educators do, this group of teachers and administrators responded with kind and humble sentiments such as, "Because I am here growing in my profession," or "I am important because we have created this opportunity for teachers to grow." While all the twenty or more responses were very well intentioned, very few tapped into their *why*. I can honestly say that not one of the teachers or administrators thought about their *why*.

When we love and care for ourselves we have thought intentionally about our *why*. As a group of educators, the *why* of their lives should be readily available and ripe for sharing. That *why* may come from any one of the areas of giving to others, service to families, community building, the love of children, and/or simply helping people become better people. Remembering that as leaders self-love is critical to our success and part of that love is understanding our why. Our why gives us meaning and purpose and fills our vessels to be more effective leaders.

In addition to knowing our why, let us not forget about the importance of service and giving. As we move forward in our leadership journeys, whether at home or in the boardroom, we must be intentional about mentally framing our work as a service and giving to others. One of the key ways we feed our souls is through the services and connectedness to those we lead and serve. As leaders, when we spend our time and our intellectual resources helping others grow, we are serving others. We are infusing and sharing our strengths and resources with others in an effort to support their growth and accomplishments so they can, in turn, give their resources to others. Oftentimes we don't take the time to examine our actions, thoughts, and motives, and while we are moving ahead with our work or actions we fail to recognize or frame our actions as a form of service or giving. We may just *do* without recognizing the impact that our doing has. Being intentional about reviewing our thoughts and actions is important as we love and care for ourselves as leaders.

When the presenter asked the teachers and administrators why they were important, not one mentioned their service to others. And while I empathize with being put on the spot, it is sad that a group of educators has not come to appreciate their service and giving to their students and their community. In their daily work of teaching and serving students, the intentional mental framing of their contributions has not taken place. Taking the time to reflect and intentionally define their work and importance had been left aside for the actual work itself. As leaders let us care for ourselves by being intentional about our mindset, mind frames and the way we look at our efforts. The way we choose to frame our work and the mindsets we choose to define our actions is vital in defining our mission and finding a meaningful life.

Beyond intentionally knowing our why and preparing our mental frames, loving ourselves includes creating mindful habits that allow us to increase our self-awareness and strengthen our rational thinking.[20] Taking time to mentally prepare ourselves for the demands of leadership is a careful and intentional undertaking that not only rewards others but helps to improve our own mental health and well-being. In addition to mindfulness, we have covered the intentional habits of yoga, supporting our bodies with healthy eating and exercise, journaling, and acts of kindness. As leaders in the workplace, in the community, and in our homes, being intentional toward our well-being is vitally important to filling our cups and keeping ourselves healthy and productive. In terms of self-care, while there is a large chasm between knowledge and action, there must be an intentional drive toward ensuring the ingredients for well-being are in our day-to-day lives.

Intentionally caring for and loving the minds and bodies that we have been designed to encapsulate is an act of honoring the creator. For example, take for a moment the notion that we regularly care for and maintain the cars we drive. We spend hundreds of dollars each year cleaning and maintaining our mode of transportation. We have the oil changed regularly and ensure the fluids are clean and at the appropriate levels. We change the brakes when necessary and make sure the car's systems are working appropriately. Why do we do this? Because we value the use of the vehicle. It allows us to move about as we choose. It allows us to get to and from work and even take a road trip when we like. It provides us a great service and in return we care for it. How much more should we be intentional about caring for our own minds and bodies. While we embody these

---

[20]Thomas Armstrong, *Mindfulness in the Classroom: Strategies for Promoting Concentration, Compassion, and Calm* (ASCD, 2019).

natural machines in which we live, might it be a valuable venture to care for the machine we have been given? It should be cared for and nurtured, cleaned and maintained mentally, spiritually, and physically. Being intentional about our well-being is an act of self-love, and in the rest of this chapter we will explore some of the elements of well-being in an effort to ensure their inclusion in our lives.

Well-Being: Positive Moments

When I was a child, I remember waking up on so many occasions with this immense feeling of joy and excitement. Let me briefly share a quick picture of my childhood. I did not grow up in wealth or live anything close to an extravagant life. I grew up in a middle-class community. I was from a divorced family, my mother struggled to put food on the table and clothes on the backs of both myself and my brother and sister. We were blessed to live in a diverse little community outside Chicago with many great schools and wonderful families. Generally speaking, I lived a relatively traditional middle-class lifestyle. We stayed in the same house my entire childhood, and it was in this world I experienced these awesome sensations of joy and hope.

I think much of the reason I had such experiences was the anticipation of doing something fun and exciting. As a boy, I had no shortage of energy, and I was always excited to be out playing sports, riding my bike, or playing capture the flag with my friends. In my early teens me and my friends would ride our skateboards and hang out at the arcade, skate shop or just go get a Slurpee from the local convenience store. These experiences were simple, yet they brought me so much joy and excitement.

I remember a time when I was in eighth grade when I had a really fun experience that has lived in my mind for years. I had a friend who was selling a little motorcycle and he was willing to part with it for just fifty bucks. When I was in eighth grade, I did odd jobs around the neighborhood, so I was able to scrape together fifty dollars for this little bike. Looking back, it was a piece of junk, but when I had the opportunity to buy this little bike there was no way I was going to turn it down. This was going to be a larger-than-life experience for me and in my mind this little bike was my ticket to freedom. I could envision myself cruising the neighborhood at my leisure. I could go wherever I wanted. This little bike was going to open up the world for me. This bike was really going to elevate my status among my friends and the girls. This was a real win for me.

I went over to my friend's house to buy the bike. I gave him my fifty bucks and that piece of rusted metal and rubber was mine. I sat down on this beauty, envisioning my newfound freedom and started the engine. It purred like a kitten (with a hacking cough). No matter, it was mine. So I clicked this little monster into first gear and let go of the clutch and started to move forward. I then started to move faster and faster, and not having ever ridden a motorcycle failed to understand the basic start and stop mechanisms of the bike. I proceeded to move forward at full force with no understanding of how to stop until I found the first thing that was going to force my stoppage. I had smashed full force into a parked car trailer. I flew sideways into this massive heap of metal cutting my shoulder deep.

In my embarrassment and pain, I lifted the bike up. I had bent the front fork, and the steering was now off center, but I got back on that thing with a bit more caution and learned to ride that beauty. And after dealing with a little blood and some bruising, my dream had come true. I spent the summer riding around the neighborhood on that thing, and I loved it. I would cruise to my friends' houses all around the area and even got chased by the cops once. It was a very exciting experience and gave me a lot of joy.

Beyond this experience, I can remember so many fun and joyous moments as a kid, and that feeling I had woken up with so many times was the result of the hope and joy of knowing I was going to have some positive experiences in my day. Dr. Martin Seligman, father of today's positive psychology movement, posits that well-being occurs when people have positive experiences in their lives.[21] When people actively seek out positive experiences in their lives, they are tending to their well-being, and they lead happier, healthier lives.

---

[21]Martin Seligman, *Flourish: A Visionary New Understanding of Happiness and Well-Being* (New York: Simon and Schuster, 2012).

While my motorcycle experience back in eighth grade certainly did give me joy, there are a lot of little ways to infuse positive moments into each of our lives and they don't have to be major happenings. They can be simple moments that elevate our mood, add pride to our lives, or maybe connect us with others. Organizational psychologist Dean Heath asserts that meaningful, remarkable, and memorable moments have specific characteristics that elevate us, ensue pride, connect us to others, and lead to insightfulness.[22] Positive moments that lead to personal well-being have those same qualities. Positive moments lead us to joy and hope, and being intentional about their inclusion in our lives is vital to our happiness.

Much like the mindsets and habits, which we discussed in chapter 3, being intentional and habitual about our positive moments is our responsibility. ***Intentionality is the cost of admission to a happier more meaningful life, and making positive moments happen in our lives is vital.*** There are many opportunities to create positive moments in our lives, and the possibilities are endless, not to mention that each person may find beauty in experiences that are unique only to themselves. I have a colleague who finds great joy in the simple moments of making breakfast in his mobile home. He will take his mobile home and drive ten minutes from his house to camp for the night just to wake up in nature and have coffee and breakfast outside. These are his positive moments.

I have another colleague who has created an annual dads' camping trip. He and other fathers all get together with their children and have a beautiful camping weekend with their kids. It is a time of connection and togetherness. They play games and have little competitions. They enjoy cooking out and breaking bread together. It is a moment of elevation and connection, and it has strengthened families and friendships.

Other moments can be simple. You can plant a garden and tend to its growth. Writing is a beautiful way to spend some moments. Reading can also be a quiet and peaceful moment of insight and growth. Taking walks or maybe even a bike ride can be another way to find

---

[22]Chip Heath and Dan Heath, *The Power of Moments: Why Certain Experiences Have Extraordinary Impact* (New York: Simon and Schuster, 2017).

a beautiful experience. While these moments can be simple and easy to find in your daily or weekly calendar, let's not forget about being intentional about the positive moments we spend with our friends and loved ones.

When we are creating positive moments, it is also important that we ensure that we spend time connected to others, especially to those whom we are closest. Being intentional about seeing and spending time with those who add joy to our lives is something we can often let slide. For our well-being, we must inventory those people who are positive additions to our lives to make sure that we are seeing them on occasion. People who are positive, loving, and caring lead to positive experiences in our lives, and connecting with them can be a simple and great way to just have a little fun.

In addition to the simple and connected experiences, don't be afraid to go big once in a while for things that elevate your human experience. Maybe you love travel, concerts, musicals, or plays. Maybe you are a fan of going to the beach or hiking through the mountains. Maybe you love sports, and seeing your favorite team is a great experience for you. Whatever it may be, being intentional about building these positive experiences into your life supports your well-being. It is an act of care and self-love, and it will allow you to have moments of elevation, insight, connectedness, and purpose.

Engagement

I was recently watching a US Open tennis match, and for me that is a rarity. I know that some love the game; however, I have never quite found the hook that grabbed my attention for tennis. Thus, watching tennis has never occupied any of my free time. On this particular Saturday evening, however, things were different. The commentators were talking about a new American phenom who was about to take the spotlight. They were bringing this young tennis player to life for those of us watching on TV. They made us feel more closely connected to her, her family, and her story. Many of the spectators in the stadium were adorning her branded T-shirts and there was a sense of excitement around this new player.

She was to be playing against the number-one seed in the tournament, and her opponent was tough. The story line was a proverbial David versus Goliath, and her opponent who was going to be tough to take down. As this young phenom walked onto the court, she had an air of confidence, and she looked focused and ready for the match. Her opponent was certainly ready to play as well, and she was not taking this new competitor lightly. As the match started, the young phenom stumbled and went down the first three sets. She did not waver in her determination, however. In set four, she dished out a 119-mile-per-hour serve that shocked me. This young lady looked so very young, and I was astonished that that little human could pull off a serve with such velocity. It was at this point that I was intrigued and googled this young lady. She was fifteen years old! I could not believe it. I was astounded that this US Open competitor was so young and was matching up with the best in the world.

As match four played out, the young phenom was growing more confident. She quickly won set four and was onto win another. In set five, she again responded ferociously to her opponent and you could see her confidence continue to grow. Her belief in herself was palpable, and after a few winning fist pumps I really began to find myself rooting for this young lady. When the match was tied 3–3, I thought, *Wow, could this fifteen-year-old really take down the number-one seed*? It was an exciting match, and the competition was something awesome to watch. I felt as if I was seeing history take place, and I was experiencing the awakening of a new giant in women's tennis.

While ultimately the number-one seed would prevail, I have to say I was *engaged*. I had lost track of time. My attention was solely focused on this match to the point where my awareness was nowhere other than the television screen. The story connected to my heart, my mind, my competitive spirit, and I was hooked. The notion that this young fifteen-year-old tennis player could take down the number one seed gave me a feeling of excitement and hope for this young lady. The fans in the stands wearing T-shirts captured my sense of team and drew me into a connection with this player. After an hour had gone by, I had to wonder where it went. I was so focused on this match I had forgotten about time. My attention was zeroed in, and I was completely *engaged* in this event.

When we are intentional about our well-being, we seek out moments of engagement. Those moments of engagement can come from many places and have unlimited effects on our hearts and minds. Mihaly Csikszentmihalyi termed this state of being totally immersed in an activity, devoid of ego and self-awareness, a state of *flow*.[23] This state of engagement, *flow*, exists when our hearts and minds are deeply steeped in an activity that has a connection and challenge to who we are and the skills we bring to the table. As leaders being focused on our well-being, we are charged with being engaged in our work, in our personal lives, and in our communities. And reaching this state of flow, when channeled toward the right activities, can be very rewarding.

Have you ever played a sport? Maybe you were a tennis, soccer, football, baseball, or softball player? If so, you can relate. When athletes step into the game, they reach this state of engagement. They are completely focused on the game. They engage all their senses and lose track of self being completely zeroed in on the competition. When a player reaches that state of flow, they have used all their athletic skills to focus on the challenge at hand. It is here where we come into a state of total immersion and loss of self.

Athletics is not the only arena in which we can reach a state of flow. In our work, we may also experience this deep sense of engagement as well. Maybe you have been in a situation in which your skills and your challenges have met to allow you to reach peak performance. You may have been leading a meeting in which you were completely prepared and knowledgeable. You were firing on all cylinders, and after the meeting you realized that time had seemingly flown by, and your meeting met its mark.

People also find themselves in a state of flow when they are reaching their creative potentials. Writers, musicians, artists, architects, designers, and other creative minds find that they reach a state of flow when they are completely immersed in their work and their minds are focused on creating something new. The act of creativity draws the author so deeply into the experience that they lose themselves while their attention is focused squarely on the design.

---

[23]Nakamura, J., and Csikszentmihalyi, M. (2014). The concept of flow. In *Flow and the foundations of positive psychology* (239–263). Springer, Dordrecht.

In Daniel Pink's book *Drive*, he states that "In flow, people lived so deeply in the moment, and felt so utterly in control, that their sense of time, place, and even self melted away. They were autonomous, of course. But more than that, they were *engaged*."[24] Do you know that feeling? Have you had moments in your past when your challenges so beautifully met your skill set that you became lost in the moment? Creating moments of engagement in our lives is just another way in which we intentionally tend to our well-being. When we are leaders who are focused on being our best selves, we must be driven to create engaging life experiences. Leaders need to be thoughtful about the activities that lead to a state of flow and engagement and capitalize on those activities to make an impact in our work. When we reach our state of flow, we know we have found the marriage between our skills and our motivations, and we have found a place where we can make a positive impact in our lives and for others.

Meaning in Something Larger than Yourself

I want to take this section to talk about finding meaning in this life and the power that fills our hearts and minds when we find ourselves living for something greater than ourselves. While I mentioned earlier that I am not intending there to be a religious focus in this book, I will not discount the power of spirituality in our lives. In Donald Miller's book *A Million Miles in a Thousand Years*, he makes a profound statement that we are "trees in a story about a forest."[25] This resonant statement reminds us that the larger story is not about us, but about our contribution to the larger story. When we recognize that the forest was created not by us or for us, we start to connect more deeply with the creator of that forest. There is a divine power that challenges us to use our lives in ways that support the growth and beauty of the forest the divine power created. When we are intentional about our well-being, we seek to connect to something larger and more meaningful than ourselves, and we seek to contribute to the beauty of humanity by using our skills, gifts, and talents. We tend to the forest of our creator.

---

[24]Daniel H. Pink, *Drive: The Surprising Truth About What Motivates Us* (New York: Penguin Press, 2011).
[25]Donald Miller, *A Million Miles in a Thousand Years: What I Learned While Editing My Life* (Nashville, TN: Thomas Nelson, 2009).

While attending a conference recently, a well-respected and experienced colleague was giving the keynote speech. Simply put, the topic focused on self-care and balancing life with work and family priorities. My colleague is in his late sixties, and he has had a very successful career as a superintendent of a large school district in Illinois. He dedicated years of his life to high-level schooling and community service; however, when he spoke that afternoon, he wasn't talking about his life from the lens of hard work or community service. He didn't talk about the importance of getting to the office early and being the last to leave. He didn't stress working himself to the bone. No, this was not his motive for talking with this group of highly educated, aspiring achievers. When he spoke, he spoke softly, and he spoke with intention about the power faith had on his life. Despite all the accolades and his successes, his story was about connecting to something more meaningful than himself.

His story was powerful. He shared how he had been working hard and burning the candle at both ends, so to speak. He had been working long days and late nights, and although he was taking care of himself physically, he was not prioritizing his family or his faith. Then he shared how one day, five years earlier, he had experienced a driving pain in his chest. He found himself on the floor writhing in pain. He was taken by ambulance to the hospital, where they discovered he had experienced a pulmonary embolism. While on the hospital bed, however, he had had an adverse reaction to the medications the doctors provided, and he went into cardiac arrest. For several minutes, his heart had stopped. They were able to revive him with electric shock, but his heart failed two more times. All three times he was able to be revived with electric shock treatment. As he shared the story, you could feel in his voice and see in his eyes that he was shaken. This episode changed his perspective of the world, his life, his faith, and his work. This moment in his life changed the way he viewed the world and how he would reclaim his faith. After this incident, he decided he was going to realign his priorities and put his faith and his family first. He shared how he would no longer take things for granted and how his level of gratitude grew immensely. He spoke about his love for his family, and the thought of not being there for his grandkids was frightening. With all that he shared, he concluded with the divine, and how this incident ignited his connection to God and his faith, and in that connection his life has greater meaning and fulfillment. His faith has become the center of his well-being, and he is intentionally focused on his God.

We hear stories like this often. It takes situations like these to rattle our cages and get us thinking about what is ultimately important in our lives. When we care for ourselves, we place our spiritual lives at the center and let all else grows from there. Much like we rely on the overwhelming power of the sun to fuel all life on earth, when we put the divine at the center, its power ignites all the other areas of our life, including our work, our relationships, and how we use our talents and resources.

Stephen Covey, author of *The 7 Habits of Highly Effective People*, concludes his best-selling book with a personal note that reads as follows:

> As I conclude this book, I would like to share my own personal conviction concerning what I believe to be the source of correct principles. Correct principles are natural laws, and God, the Creator and Father of us all, is the source of them and also the source of our conscience. I believe that to the degree people live by this inspired conscience, they will grow to fulfil their natures; to the degree that they do not, they will not rise above the animal plane.
>
> I believe there are parts of human nature that cannot be reached by either legislation or education, but require the power of God to deal with. I believe that as human beings, we cannot perfect ourselves. To the degree to which we align ourselves with correct principles, divine endowments will be released within our nature in enabling us to fulfill the measure of our creation. In the words of Teilhard de Chardin, "We are not human beings having a spiritual experience. We are spiritual beings having a human experience."

I found this statement to be very profound for three reasons. *The 7 Habits* has sold over twenty-five million copies and has become universally known as an effective manual for personal and organizational success. Knowing the success of the book, what I find profound is the position in which this statement resides. This statement is his last statement in the book and serves to be his concluding remarks. Essentially, this statement serves to contextualize all the other precepts of the book as being principles that are effective to the degree to which we align our lives to something divine. After Covey shares the well-researched habits of highly effective people, I find it significant that he would conclude with the notion that our measure of fulfillment will be directly aligned to our connection to God. In no uncertain terms, Covey drives home the point on his last page that our personal effectiveness will be directly linked to the measure in which we are connected to God.

Secondly, Covey points out that he believes God is the source of our consciousness—that is, God creates our self-awareness. As beings who are uniquely aware of ourselves, the intentional drive for our own personal well-being is paramount in leading meaningful and fulfilling lives. When we are aware of ourselves, and we respect the idea that we are connected to a creator that is larger than ourselves, we experience a beautiful perspective on life and a deep sense of contentment. If we view our lives as being a part of something much larger than ourselves, connected to the divine, we find meaning, beauty, and love. Embracing the divine gives our lives a much deeper meaning and also reminds us that we are that tree in that story about a forest. We *are* living in a symbiotic existence with ourselves and our creator.

Finally, I want to touch upon Covey's idea that to the degree we align ourselves with God's principles will be our measure of fulfillment. God wants us to love ourselves. He wants us to love our neighbors. When we align ourselves to these very basic principles, it leads to greater engagement in our lives, meaning in our stories, and fulfillment in our purpose. Our connection to the principles that God has laid out for us, how we are to treat people, and how we are to treat ourselves are not overly religious ideas. They are spiritual ideas. They are the ideas of the heart. When we align our lives to these principles, we will be living for more than ourselves, and we will be living for the divine.

When we live a life of intentional well-being, we are aware and focused on including the divine in our lives. To live for something more than yourself is to support your neighbor and yourself. It is to live a life for humanity and to embrace using your gifts and talents for the greater good. As leaders, caring for yourself is vital to bringing your best self to the arena every day, and when you come to the arena alongside the Spirit, your leadership will have meaning and new purpose for yourself and those you lead.

Please let me say here I am not endorsing any religion or organized religious institution. I am talking about being connected to the eternal spirit that lives in the heart of people, that drives us toward what is good and beautiful in this world.

Being Connected to One Another

We know that being intentional about being connected to something larger than ourselves is instrumental to our well-being because we were created to be connected. Not only were we wired to be connected to a higher power but we were also created to be connected to one another. We are social beings and the benefits of being relationally and emotionally connected to others are vast. Research shows that people who are more closely connected with others experience physical benefits such as a healthier immune system and less illness. They are also emotionally healthier and experience less stress and anxiety. We also know that people who have strong connections in their lives are also able to change negative patterns of behavior and live more productive lives.[26]

As leaders who are intentional about our well-being, we must give care and attention to fostering high-quality relationships, not only for ourselves but also for those we lead. Creating environments that support healthy relationships in our organization leads to improved results and organizational success. When we are intentional about nurturing high-quality relationships, we not only experience organizational benefits but we also experience deep personal satisfaction as well. When we come to the leadership table having

---

[26]Henry Cloud, *The Law of Happiness: How Ancient Wisdom and Modern Science Can Change Your Life* (New York: Simon and Schuster, 2011).

deep and meaningful connections in our own lives, we are better able to give to others out of our fullness.

When our lives include high-quality connections, we experience a sense of belonging and connectedness. These connections actually increase our serotonin and oxytocin levels giving us positive feelings of contentment and happiness. By intentionally establishing connections in our lives, we are actually impacting our physiological selves to have increased life satisfaction and well-being. So, while there are certainly some very noticeable benefits in having positive relationships, we now know that there are also biological and chemical benefits as well. The point is this: if we want to experience our best life, both personally and professionally, we must be intentional about establishing high-quality relationships in our lives.

Principles of Connection: Understanding Purpose and Setting Parameters

In order to establish high-quality relationships, there are some principles we can follow that can lead us to healthy and strong connections. Let's start with purpose and parameters. We have many people in our lives. We have loved ones, friends, family, colleagues, business partners, acquaintances, and the like. Each of these relationships occupies a certain place in our minds and in our hearts. Our family and close friends are often associated with love, care, security and belonging. These relationships tend to be our closest and we tend to nurture and care for them more regularly. These relationships give us a sense of togetherness and protection, and when healthy, tend to be the foundation of our social world. The purpose for these relationships is often love, growth, care, nurturing, socializing, fun and play. Loved ones and family require the greatest investments on our part. This may include all our resources, such as time, money, and social-emotional investments. These relationships are highly valuable, and when they are positive we tend to feel and experience their benefits. On the other hand, when they are damaged or toxic, we tend to experience their negative impacts, feelings, and emotions.

Other relationships exist in our lives as well. These relationships are more loosely connected to our hearts and minds but still carry importance and meaning in our lives. Those may be colleagues, far off acquaintances or even some distant friends and family. The relationships with colleagues may tend to be more transactional and there may be less emotional connection. These relationships may include care and thoughtfulness but may be less about love. These relations can often include a social exchange—that is, their purpose is to complete a task, achieve an outcome, or to give and get something in return. These relationships also require significant investments. Connections with colleagues require social connection and trust building. These relationships are very valuable for the purpose and mission of the organization and our attention to them is critical.

In regards to far-off acquaintances and family, these may be loose connections that exist due to the nature of time or distance. These may be people you know but their inclusion in your life may be minimal and your mutual investments in these relationships may be nominal. What is important here is simply recognizing the relationship we have in our lives. There are many types of relationships in our lives and their purposes vary along with their required investments. While I briefly describe relationships here, it should also be noted that sometimes these relationships overlap and don't fit nicely into the little boxes I've described. Nonetheless, it is important for us to recognize and intentionally inventory the relationship that we do have, their role in our lives, and the investments we must make to support them.

In addition to recognizing the relationships in our lives, we must also be intentional about the parameters we must set on each of them. Cloud and Townsend, in their best-selling book *Boundaries*, share the importance of setting boundaries for each of our relationships in order for them to grow and thrive. They posit that healthy relationships have clearly established rules and parameters, which support authenticity and freedom. To explain, let me share a hypothetical example.

Suppose you have a wonderful friend. She is a person with whom you have shared memories and good times. You often find yourselves enjoying dinners together while having meaningful conversation.

On occasion, you see a movie, concert, or play together and maybe have a little wine and painting night. You know the type of friends I am talking about! Now imagine this person whom you care for and share a deep, meaningful connection decides she wants to move into your home with you and spend a few months having more of those fun times together, and you agree. Do you think that changing the parameters or boundaries of that relationship may change the relationship? Do you see there being a potential for a very different type of relationship?

Let's imagine how things might change. One day you might wake up, and she is in the kitchen having coffee in the seat you often sit in. She may have the TV on watching the morning news, where you may prefer to quietly read and meditate in the morning. OK, you can handle that—just a mild inconvenience. Then she makes breakfast and leaves all the dishes in the sink. No problem—she will get to them later. When you get home from the office, however, those dishes are still there. OK, deep breath. This will work out. After staring at the crusty dishes, you then go to do a load of laundry, but the washing machine is full of wet clothes. So, being kind, you throw them in the dryer for your beloved friend. When she gets home, she informs you that the clothes you threw in the dryer needed to be hung, not dried! You can see where I am going with this. While she is a friend, and you care for her deeply, your friendship contains certain operational boundaries or parameters. You do certain things together and avoid others. This is normal and natural in relationships. People who are not intentional about understanding the nature of their relationships and appropriate boundaries will allow themselves or others to be boundary busters. When boundaries are broken, we know it. How? We will feel it! Going back to the example, how might you feel about this friend after a few weeks of having her around every day? You might feel annoyed, angered, and may prefer your friend move back to her place!

Being intentional about our relational connections requires us to know the nature of our relationships and set appropriate boundaries. While this is not intended to be a dictation about establishing appropriate boundaries, I can promise you, when you have them in your life you will find deeper meaning and

freedom in your relationships. Healthy, meaningful, mature relationships include an understanding and respect for where the relationship begins and ends.

Principles of Connection: Attention and Understanding

Human connectedness and high-quality relationships also require focused attention, genuine empathy, and a deep understanding of one another. In order for humans to really connect and experience the benefits of quality relationships, they need to give attention to those they are choosing to spend time with. Daniel Goleman, author of *Emotional Intelligence*, claims that today, due to technology, our attention is under assault.[27] And I think you may agree. Do a little experiment next time you go out to eat or go to a restaurant. Take notice of how many people are staring at their cell phones while in the company of others. All too often I have seen couples, children and parents, and colleagues sit down to share a meal while being preoccupied with their cell phones while in the company of others.

Just recently I saw a couple in their thirties eating breakfast at a local pancake house. Both stared at their cell phones the entire time they were dining, only to look up when one of their mothers came in. Ordinarily, you might expect that the mother would grab an extra seat and join this not so deeply engaged couple. Nope! The mother sat at the table next to them by herself and also read from her cell phone! Needless to say, none of these three was attempting to connect with any of the others.

Unfortunately, this is not uncommon, and I am sure you have seen this yourself. Too often people are so focused on other things that they are missing out on deep connections with one another. When we attempt to build and experience the benefits of relationships, we must draw our attention to the other person. When connecting with others, it is imperative that we seek to gain an understanding of *their* thoughts, feelings, and perspectives. Have you ever been speaking to someone and in your conversation you can clearly see they are distracted or not paying attention to you? When you

---

[27]Daniel Goleman, *Emotional Intelligence* (New York: Bantam Books, 2005).

experience this do you feel engaged with the other person? Do you feel a connection to that person? Most likely not. Interactions such as these are transactional and do not foster connection. Connection occurs when we as individuals are intentional about our relatedness, therefore, focusing our attention on the other in order to seek understanding.

In Stephen Covey's best seller, *7 Habits of Highly Effective People*, he posits that if we want to be effective in our relationships, either at home or at the office, we have to seek to understand before we are understood. His precept here is that if we expect to develop meaningful, high-quality relationships we have to be able to understand the other person. In doing so, we need to focus our attention on intentional understanding—that is, we need to draw our minds and our attention to the other person in order to comprehend their personhood.

Do you have friends or family who truly understand you? Do you have people who know how you will react to certain situations? People who can finish your sentences? These people have experienced you and have been able to understand you. As you seek to care for yourself as a leader, developing deep meaningful connections with others is vital to your well-being and contentment. Being intentionally focused on connecting with others will support and fill your life with high-quality relationships.

Principles of Connection: Building Emotional Connections

As we care for ourselves and our well-being, we know that developing and fostering relationships in our lives serves to lead to a healthier and happier life. People who are emotionally and relationally connected experience a greater quality of life and report higher levels of life satisfaction. As we approach our work, our home lives, and our lives within our communities, our ability to support and strengthen our relationships will pay dividends for the people we choose to serve and lead. While tending to relationships and recognizing appropriate boundaries are important ingredients in our relational recipe, equally important is tending to the emotional quality of those relationship. Stephen Covey refers to this as the emotional bank account. He propounds that each of our relationships holds a sort of an imaginary bank account, in which each member of the relationship makes both deposits and withdrawals. People make investments in relationships through time, attention, love and understanding. On the other hand, people can make withdrawals by disrupting boundaries, making demands, exhibiting aggressive behaviors, or any number of exploits that can place pressure on a relationship. While withdrawals don't always have to be negative, being thoughtful and careful about them is necessary and must be counterbalanced with greater deposits in the relationship.

The emotional bank account that supports healthy and meaningful relationships can be seen in every arena, at home or in the office, and it can be easily understood through our deepest connections. Let me share an example of my relationship with my now-twenty something daughter. As my daughter was growing up, we spent a lot of time together. There was play and fun. There was care and attention. We spent hours reading together, talking, and relating. She was (and always will be) daddy's little girl. We spent nearly every summer on the beach enjoying vacations together and expressed lots of love toward one another. As she got older, however, like many children, she began to develop a stronger sense of self and independence. There were times when she needed to be taught, corrected, or redirected. This is not uncommon for teens who are growing and learning. For her, however, these were seemingly unpleasant redirections. For example, when my daughter was a late teen she chose to quit her job. She did not have a solid reason for quitting, other than it wasn't enjoyable. She did not discuss this with me prior to quitting, and she did not having a plan in place to find another job. In doing so, she thought I would support her dwindling bank account by providing her with money for her expenses and recreational activities. Boy, was she mistaken. Instead, I allowed her to experience the consequences of her poor decision by removing her allowance. She did not like my response to her quitting her job. Not only was she without her own income but she was no longer getting my allowance either. In her eyes, this was a major withdrawal! I thought this was just solid parenting! Either way, she didn't like it.

But despite the fact that I removed her allowance and placed a burden on her finances, our relationship remained very strong. Why? Because of the investments made during her childhood and beyond. With so much time and love invested in our relationship, when it came time to make a proverbial withdrawal, the bank account was so enriched that the funds were barely missed. Parenthetically, if I do say so myself, I thought this was a good lesson in responsible decision-making. I'm still not sure she agrees!

Invest in Quality Time

When we view our relationships through the lens of this figurative bank account, we can begin to be more intentional about how we invest in our relationships at home, with our friends, and with our colleagues. If we value our own well-being and want to improve the relationships in our lives, we need to make relational investments. When we choose to support the relationships in our lives, we need to carve out time to support and foster those relationships. When caring for our loved ones and our closest friends and colleagues, we have to be deliberate about setting up times to connect. For example, I have a dear friend who I only see once a year because of our busy calendars. We intentionally carved out time each year to set up a dinner where we share stories, talk about our families, and have a few laughs. We are purposeful about this date and often joke about it saying, "OK, see ya next year!" And although we only see each other sparingly, we both cherish our friendship; therefore we have been intentional about this date each and every year for the last decade. We make time for us.

In addition to carving our time, we must support our relationships through empathy and understanding—that is, we need to really seek to care for those we love by listening intently and giving our full hearts and minds to our relationship. Again, in our once-a-year meeting, my friend and I put our phones away, and we share stories about our lives, our friends, our work, and our loved ones. The time may be short, and it may only be once a year, but we are intentional about our listening and our understanding of one another. This one simple act has created a beautiful friendship that gives us both mutual edification.

Make Time for Play

As we support the relational connections in our lives by investing in our emotional and relational bank accounts, we also need to take time to just enjoy our relationships through acts of play. Play allows us to strengthen our emotional connections and build high-quality relationships at both work and home. When we allow room for play within our relationships, it gives space for us to get into a state of flow, in which we can lose our sense of self and just focus on a game or activity together. Research supports that when we engage in play it helps to build positive feelings and connections among one another. Play gives us a sense of relinquishing our normal roles and expectations and allows individuals to relate with a sense of freedom and happiness.[28]

One organization I have worked with makes play a regular part of their routines and rituals in order to create a greater sense of connection and camaraderie among employees. This organization regularly celebrates its success through themed parties where the members of the organization dress up in costumes or team T-shirts and the like, in order to have a little fun and express their solidarity and connectedness. Teams within the organization try to outdo one another through some friendly competition by dressing up in fun and goofy ways to celebrate their work and bring a sense of playfulness to the group.

Friends, family, and colleagues often build and strengthen connections by engaging in other playful activities as well. A perfect example: on any given summer weekend, all across America you will find droves of people playing golf together. Golf has served to support countless personal, political, and business relationships across the decades. Some of our greatest American presidents have made significant foreign policy deals and economic connections by engaging in the playful act of golf. Why has golf served to build such profound economic and political relationships? Because when we engage in play we allow ourselves to connect in new ways and this fun and playfulness can lead to stronger high-quality relationships.

---

[28]Stephens, J. P., Heaphy, E., and Dutton, J. E. (2012). "High-quality connections." *The Oxford handbook of positive organizational scholarship*, 385–399.

In sum, remember, as leaders, high-quality relationships are not only good for others but they are also extremely important for us. As we seek to strengthen ourselves and fill our vessels, intentionally tending to high-quality relationships will serve to improve our well-being and the overall quality of our lives. Let's not forget that building quality relationships takes focus and effort. It requires us to think about the basis of our relationships, as each of our connections is unique, and carries a unique purpose. Further, relationships require focused time and attention—that is, relationships do not grow without our proverbial watering and fertilization. As we care for our relationships and recognize their importance in our lives and our well-being, let us also not forget to establish the healthy boundaries that support mutual connectedness, understanding, and freedom. Our human connections are the lifeblood of our hearts and souls. As humans we were never meant to live in isolation and being intentional about supporting our connections will serve to fill our cups, giving us the strength and care to serve our neighbors, colleagues, friends, and loved ones.

Finding Small Wins

Beyond building positive relationships, creating meaning in our lives, enjoying positive experiences, and deeply engaging in life, well-being theory posits that achievement leads to a more flourishing life[29]. Achievement, simply put, is the realization of our goals. It is the successful completion of any specific task or activity that we set out to accomplish. And while this may seem oversimplified, the inclusion of accomplishments in our lives serves to lead us to a more positive life experience. I will also add that the feelings that often accompany accomplishment can be fleeting and thus it should be noted that accomplishment in the context of a growth mindset serves to more completely support our well-being.

Let me explain. Well-being theory propounds that accomplishment in any form, however fleeting, will serve to create a more flourishing life. And while this theory is well grounded in research, I propound that when our accomplishments are part of an overall growth mindset

---

[29]Martin Seligman, *Flourish: A Visionary New Understanding of Happiness and Well-Being* (New York: Simon and Schuster, 2012).

they serve more intently to be acts of love and care for ourselves. What I mean is that accomplishment and the feelings that go along with accomplishment are often temporary. For example, when a team wins the big game they often celebrate the great accomplishment for a while, but not too long after that feeling fades and they are running after their next accomplishment. After winning the 2019 NFL Super Bowl, the New England Patriots' quarterback, Tom Brady, when standing on the winning podium being interviewed, mentioned he was already looking forward to next year and winning again. After just a few minutes, while standing on that podium immediately after winning, the feeling of accomplishment was fading, and he was thinking about the future and his next big win! In life, we have accomplishments, but we cannot rely on those temporary feelings to give us long term well-being, which is why we have to plot our accomplishments on a timeline of personal growth. A timeline that leads to a lifetime of well-being.

Obviously, not all of us will be Super Bowl winners, but life has many small victories and accomplishments along the way. We experience the joy of graduating college, landing our first big job, experiencing a promotion, getting the MBA, and moving to a leadership position. All these accomplishments live on our timeline of continual growth. And it is the timeline of continual growth that supports our overall well-being. **When we look at our lives from the lens of growth over time, with an eye on continuous improvement, we allow ourselves to celebrate our successes, and also look at the success as just one part of driving ourselves to be a little bit better every day, week, year, or decade.** Our successes are not isolated or static, but rather a part of the larger picture of our lives, where we are undergoing regular renewal and growth. Carol Dweck, author of *Mindset: The New Psychology of Success*, describes that as people, when we live life being fully open to the idea that we are not complete and that our experiences lead us to growth and learning, we are able to live a life of fulfillment and purpose. Dweck posits that maintaining a growth mindset allows us to have the freedom to know that we are not done growing but always on a path of continuous improvement and accomplishment.

Let me add some color here to illustrate. I have a friend and colleague who is a dynamic educator, speaker, and author who shares his story of growth mindset by speaking about his old track days in high school. He was a very successful cross-country runner when he was in high school and made the state tournament and set school records for the one-mile run. In his quest for cross-country dominance, he set a goal to run a four-minute mile, which, from what I understand, is a pretty amazing feat. He trained hard and eventually set the school record by running a mile in four minutes and thirty-two seconds. And while many may view this as a failure, those of us who live with a growth mindset realize that although he didn't meet the four-minute mark he grew immensely in attempting to reach that goal. The accomplishment wasn't necessarily meeting the goal; the accomplishment was all the growth that came from his effort.

I'd like to share another example that comes from the professional world, where myself and a team of leaders designed a dynamic and engaging professional culture. In nearly all the schools and districts I have worked in, I have faced significant challenges related to the culture and climate of the employees and the administrators. Most of the challenges came from a significant disconnect between the teachers and the administration. You can see this play out all the time as teachers threaten to strike for any number of reasons related to pay and benefits or class size and working conditions. Even as I am writing this, the Chicago Teachers Union is on strike. When I began my tenure in one particular district, it was embroiled in a long and arduous contract standoff. The teachers and the leadership were at odds and the culture was toxic. I was charged with improving employee engagement and creating a culture of trust and collaboration.

After a long uphill climb my first year, I surveyed the teachers and gathered data related to the culture and climate improvements that occurred within the first twelve months of my tenure in the organization. I then put in place a small focus group to gather further information related to the historical toxicity of the district. With each following year, I continued to make small incremental improvements in the leadership, systems, norms, and professional behaviors within the organization that led to an over 95 percent engagement rate. Teachers and administrators were enjoying improved relations, union contracts were complete without strike and the organization was thriving. Each year, as the leadership and the union grew together, we were able to see small incremental improvements in employee engagement. While I and the teachers enjoyed the accomplishment, I did not rest after a year but kept driving forward to achieve small incremental growth over time. These small wins led to a deep sense of accomplishment and pride within me and the leaders we developed through the process. It wasn't just one accomplishment that led to our well-being, it was the path of continuous improvement that led to a long-standing sense of well-being. As leaders, we must celebrate our accomplishments, and also remember that each of them builds on one another for our personal fulfillment.

It should also be noted in this example that I was not alone on this journey in improving this particular organization's culture and climate, and it was our collective efforts that not only led to my personal well-being but the well-being of many others. As the organization moved forward year over year, we were able to create a culture in which employees felt a sense of positivity in their work and their efforts. As mentioned earlier, servanthood and service to others builds our sense of meaning and fulfillment and creating experiences that lead to both the accomplishment of ourselves and others while also serving and improving the lives of others is a dose of well-being that will fill our cups. As you move forward in your leadership journey, focusing first on your personal well-being and the well-being of others, finding opportunities for collective accomplishment is a win-win.

Summary

Imagine a life in which you go to work every day with a sense of purpose. You know your *why*. Your organization may be producing a product or providing a service that helps others to enjoy their lives and you have taken the time to intentionally frame how your work impacts others. Or maybe you lead a department, and you realize now that your leadership and service is vital in supporting the well-being of others. My point here is that you have intentionally framed your work with a sense of purpose and servanthood.

Now imagine you have put in place some of the important elements of self-care. You are taking time to read, meditate, and/or pray. Your day starts off with healthy eating and you are putting in a few workouts a week. Your body and mind are working together, and your energy levels are high and vibrant. You are also taking time to journal and write about your positive experiences and the many blessings with which you have been provided.

Finally, imagine after framing your purpose and filling your vessel with self-care, you inventory the elements of well-being that are either in your life or that you need to include. Imagine taking the time to create and reflect on positive experiences. You become intentional about building in small but positive moments into your day. You are thinking more deeply about your relationships. You ask yourself, who are the people in your life and what are the parameters of your relationships? You take time to nurture positive relationships in your life and intentionally connect with people whom you share mutual love and care. Further, you are seeking engaging experiences in both your personal and professional life. You are reaching that state of flow on occasions and are enjoying the ride. And while you have done all that is mentioned here you are growing and thriving. You are growing and getting just a little bit better every day. Is this the type of life you want? Is this how you want to care for yourself? Is this how you want to design your life?

My hope for each of us is that we find a life of meaning and purpose. My hope is that we each use our time here to build ourselves in mind, body, and spirit to enable us to give and serve others. Along the way, I hope that we are deeply engaged in our work and our lives. I hope that we have beautiful connections to others and that we experience a deep sense of love for ourselves. I hope our vessels are full and overflowing and that in turn we spill out in all areas of our lives. As we leave this part of our journey together, I hope you realize you can imagine your life as you want it. If you can imagine your life full and content, you really can put in place the intentional habits that will lead to happiness and fulfillment. One step at a time—1 percent better every day.

"It's those moments of grace when we appreciate the perfection and beauty of it all. It's those moments when we feel something eternal and invincible inside us, the core of our spirit. It's the loving warmth of our relationships with family and friends. It's finding meaningful work. It's the capacity to learn and grow, to share and serve."

—*Tony Robbins*

Love in Action

- What type of positive experiences do you want to infuse in your life? What things, both big and small, can you do that will lead to those little moments of joy and happiness? What engages you? When do you lose yourself in something? What makes you reach that state of flow, and are your seeking work that matches your passion and your talents?

  - Create an experience this month, large or small, that allows you to have some fun. Further, create an experience that allows you to reach a state of flow. This could be an activity that you are passionate about and that challenges you. It could be creative, or athletic, art, music, etc.

- Have you thought deeply about your relationships? Who? Why? And have you intentionally established the boundaries that will lead to both freedom and deep connection?

  - List the five people you spend the most time with. Describe the nature of the relationship and how the relationship serves both of you. Describe any areas that may need improvement or reconsideration.

- Are you creating small wins? How are you improving yourself each and every day? What are you going to do today to make yourself 1 percent better?

  - What small activity can you being that will lead to a sense of accomplishment—daily reading, time with family at the table, exercise, etc.

- Are you connecting with something larger than yourself? Whatever it may be for you—God, the universe, Shakti—is the power of something divine lighting your soul?

    - This one is between you, your God, and your heart and soul. How you connect is in your hands, heart, and mind.

Part II

Caring for Those We Lead

Chapter

Develop Your Organizational Why

There is nothing better than being on a shared mission with extraordinary people, who can be radically truthful and radically transparent with each other.

—*Ray Dalio*

In part I, we walked through the importance of self-care and self-love. While the golden rule tells us to love our neighbor it also reminds us to love ourselves as well. When we take the time to frame our thinking and employ the habits of well-being in our lives, we are able to lead from a place of fullness and completeness. Consequently, when our cups are full we are resourced to meet the demands of leadership in any arena. In part II, we will shift our focus toward the second portion of the golden rule and place our attention on loving and caring for others within our influence.

As leaders, we are charged with meeting the ever-changing demands of our workplace, our homes, and our organizations; and we don't do it alone. We are people living and working in community with others and our ability to lead is the lifeblood of our organizations and our people. Our leadership matters, the way we lead matters, and our ability to engage those we lead will have an immense impact on the success or failure of our mission. When we put our people first and seek to design a workplace that engages minds, hearts, creativity, and personhood, we set up our organizations for success while giving others an opportunity to live full and meaningful lives. Engagement is a beautiful ingredient in our recipe for organizational success, and our work as leaders is to ensure its inclusion.

What Is Engagement?

Have you worked in an environment in which people were disengaged? It is often marked with lack of trust, commitment, or collaboration. People often lack clarity in their goals and mission and work toward unclear ends. Disengagement usually includes people finding ways to circumvent their roles. They are shopping online, checking their personal email, and looking for ways to simply get through the day so they can move on to more meaningful things in their lives. When people are disengaged, they often refer to those above them in the organization as "management," "leadership," the "bosses," a sort of faceless entity that runs and drives the organization without any genuine connection to employees. Disengagement often looks like a top-down approach in which people feel unseen, disenfranchised, and not included in meaningful collaboration or decision-making. Have you ever seen or worked in an environment like this?

In the early 2000s, I worked with an organization that was riddled with disengaged employees, and it was largely due to a disconnected leadership team that needed some real heartfelt training in building an engaged workforce. Let me explain what this looked like from within. First, communication. The leadership within itself did not meet regularly to chart progress, set goals, or manage processes. There was little attempt to seek buy-in or collaboration from those who were working on the front lines and the chasm between management and the workforce was wide and blurry. Employees couldn't speak to the overarching goals of the organization, and more so, could not understand the process. When speaking with employees, they often felt leadership was unprepared and unseen. It was a frustrating environment in which people were wide-eyed with puzzlement and certainly didn't feel as if they were ready to put their best selves toward the mission.

In contrast, I have witnessed organizations in the same industry turn around and create environments in which employees were deeply engaged, motivated. And excited about the mission. Let me share: After years of employee dissatisfaction, another organization I have worked with was able to greatly improve its employee engagement by implementing a change strategy that was laser focused on getting employees engaged. In my focus group research, I found that the organization's previous leader had been deeply untrusting of his employees and people felt stepped on and rarely in the know. People felt there was a blinding lack of communication in which information was never disseminated across the organization. It was explained that committees would often work together toward specific ends, yet those ends were not shared nor employed across the larger organization. Employees felt out of touch, and any form of change strategy was met with impotent implementation. Employees basically felt that their hard work didn't matter, had little purpose, and didn't lead to improvements.

Further in my research with this organization, I found they had failed to implement the habits and rituals of well-being across the organization. Much like we discussed in part I, relating to personal well-being, organizations also need to incorporate the habits and rituals of intentional well-being in order to create deeply engaging, meaningful, and fulfilling working environments. The organization had failed to create a clear and meaningful mission that resonated with its employees leaving employees with little sense of purpose in their work. Additionally, employees working within committees were not experiencing the small wins and accomplishments mentioned in chapter 4. The leadership of the organization was not intentional about giving its employees meaningful and exciting work, leaving them without a sense of *flow*. In turn, those on the front lines were disengaged and largely unmotivated.

The story doesn't end there, however, and this organization was able to make significant improvements by taking some very clear and intentional steps toward building an engaged workforce that was cared for and loved. First, the leadership of the organization began by developing a strategic plan that included clear and precise goals that were collaboratively developed with input from all stakeholder groups. Next, they focused on building informal and formal leadership structures within the organization that supported the sharing of decision-making among employees. By expanding the leadership capacity of employees, the organization was able to use a crowdsourced decision-making process that improved outcomes, processes, and employee engagement. Further, the leadership developed a strong team environment in which small teams of employees worked toward specific goals allowing for greatly improved collaboration and organizational cohesion. And while the leadership was strategically focused on their mission and the right organizational structures, they also made sure to have some fun and build in the elements of well-being and happiness along the way.

I have had the privilege of working with several organizations that have made improvements such as these, and in part II we will delve more deeply into the process and practices that lead to a more engaged workforce. When we care and love the people whom we lead, we are intentional about creating meaningful and engaging work. We set up the right working environment, invest in their lives and promote their happiness for the greater good of the organization and its mission. Leading with love not only serves to support us as individual leaders but it also serves to support and love those within our care. The following chapters will focus on the following components that serve to support those we lead:

- Designing a clear mission: organizations should be laser focused on what it is they are trying to achieve by setting clear goals and objectives that support the why and purpose of the organization.

- Designing strong teams: Team development is crucial toward accomplishing the organization's mission. Setting up the right structures, protocols, and relational processes leads teams to a deeper sense of collaboration, reduces employee isolation and capitalizes on relational accountability.

- Supporting organizational well-being: Much like we have to be intentional about our own personal well-being, we have to be intentional about the well-being of our organization. Supporting employee health and well-being through intentional structures, rituals and habits will pay dividends in terms of happiness and productivity.

- Building shared leadership: Support your informal and formal leadership structures through coaching and mentorship builds a foundation of trust in the form of competence and relationships.

Starting with Our Purpose

When we move from self-love to leading with love, much like our personal *why*, we need to think intensely about the *why* and purpose of our organization. The collective conscious of our organizations needs to be crystal clear about why we operate. What is our purpose, and what good do we bring to the world?

When we care for the people in our organizations, they need to know what they are in for! They need to have a commitment to the nature of the work the organization is doing as a whole and be in understanding of that mission. Too often organizations both large and small are not clear about their purpose and they leave their employees disconnected from an essential element of human motivation.

People are motivated by a sense of purpose.[30] One of the key human motivators that drives our actions is knowing that our efforts are directed by something larger than just our own motives. When connected and engaged around a larger purpose, individuals and teams are able to accomplish great things. The mission and purpose of an organization, however, cannot be vague or esoteric, it has to be clear.

---

[30]Daniel H. Pink, *Drive: The Surprising Truth About What Motivates Us* (New York: Penguin Press, 2011).

Google has a mission statement that includes: "Organize the world's information and make it universally accessible and useful." You may be familiar with google. For many, it is an internet search engine that leads people to the information they are seeking. For others, Google is so much more. Google includes document-sharing services that allow people to work together from any location. Google includes email and communication solutions. Google customers can hold web conferences and hold meetings anywhere in the world. Google also has tremendous cloud services making portable thumb drives a thing of the past. It has also moved into the cell phone game linking its web-based services to your handheld device. Google Apps for Education have changed the ways teachers and students do schooling and their Chromebooks have made technology accessible to millions of students across the county. The truly are making information universally accessible!

Google is clear about its mission and purpose, and all arms of the organization work toward that same goal across all product lines. Google employees know their purpose and their why. The mission is ubiquitous across the organization and no matter the project they are working toward making information universally accessible. Employees know their direction and people sign up for the Google mission. Google employees report high levels of engagement and satisfaction and know very well what they are working toward.

Southwest Airlines is another organization with a strong purpose. Their mission is: "The mission of Southwest Airlines is dedication to the highest quality of customer service delivered with a sense of warmth, friendliness, individual pride, and company spirit." If you have never flown Southwest, you may be missing out on just one of their quirky nuances that makes them so warm and friendly. As a company, they allow their flight attendants to have a little fun with the flight safety announcements. One of my favorite examples of their fun and friendly announcements included one flight attendant stating, "If you're flying with more than one child, after putting your own oxygen mask on, choose the child who is most economically viable!" What a laugh!

Southwest allows its employees to show a little of their individual personalities, which translates to meeting their *warm and friendly* mission. They engage their employees by putting them in a position to directly support their mission. They give them a purpose and allow them the autonomy to shine. Creating this type of environment for its employees is just one of the many reasons Southwest reports such high levels of employee satisfaction and customer loyalty.

While Southwest and Google are both decisively clear about their purpose, and both are enormously successful and lead in their industries, it should be pointed out that their purpose is focused on making the lives of others better. Both of their missions, although not explicitly stated, are about serving people to make their lives a little better. Whether that is access to information or a warm and friendly flight, each is positioned around the care for others.

As leaders of large organizations, small organizations, teams, or even families, when we are drafting a mission statement that captures our purpose from the lens of love and care for others we are tapping into the heart of humanity. Imagine if Southwest mission statement was: "The mission of Southwest is to operate in a highly efficient and cost-effective manner maximizing profit for our shareholders." Do you think that would be a charter for employee engagement? Do you think employees would rally around that cause? I would imagine not! Rather, employees need to have their hearts engaged.

At this point, you might be saying, "Not every business is designed to serve or capture hearts." You might say, "Well, my business or my team is highly technical. We don't work in the business of love and humanity." Well, let's look at National Aeronautics and Space Administration's (NASA) purpose: "As explores, pioneers, and innovators, we boldly expand frontiers in air and space to inspire and serve America and to benefit the quality of life on Earth." NASA is a highly technical organization, but the core of their *why* is to "benefit the quality of life on earth." They are making tools for space exploration with human hearts in mind!

Much like I have mentioned in part I, **our mindset and the way we frame our thinking matters**. If we intend on engaging our people in the purpose of the organization, that purpose has to speak to their hearts, the love of humanity, and serving something greater than themselves. At the heart of humanity is our hearts (pun intended), and when we can capture the hearts of our people we are better positioned to give them work that is meaningful and valuable to their personhood. Therefore, as we delve into the work of defining our purpose, our *why* for existing, we need to keep that mindset, that frame, at the forefront of our work. Also, we must recognize that developing a *why* is not the work of just one. If we want to engage our people, we must include their hearts and minds in the process of defining our why.

Developing Our *Why* Together

Taking Ownership of Our Why

Engaging people in any activity, form of work, or mission relies heavily on their willingness to participate. Tapping into their willingness to participate requires motivating people to bring themselves into the work and/or mission. In order to motivate people to participate it is necessary to create an environment in which people have a sense of ownership in the mission and purpose. Ownership is a key lever that pulls people into being motivated around a task or purpose.

As an example, many companies will offer profit sharing benefits packages to give their employees a greater sense of ownership within the company. Why? Because companies recognize that when employees feel a greater sense of ownership within the company they are more likely to perform more effectively. Financial ownership is not the only form of ownership, however, and offering people ownership by way of leadership opportunities, creative opportunities, and advising opportunities, just to name a few, supports individual ownership as well. While ownership matters when motivating employees for performance, ownership also matters when devising and creating a mission for your company, team, or community group.

Capturing the Voice of Those inside and outside
of the Organization

When we are seeking to develop our *why*, it is necessary to create ownership by giving a voice to people both inside and outside the organization. Giving people within the organization a seat at the table is critical to their ownership of the mission. Also, seeking input from those outside the organization allows us to gather the voices of those that are being served by the organization. While those inside the organization can be employees across all departments of the organization, those outside may be defined as the customers your organization serves, partner organizations, or potential focus groups.

When your people are engaged in their organizations they know the *why* of their work and they were given voice in the development of that *why*. As you develop the *why* of your organization be sure to capture the voice of your employees. Allow development meetings to occur that include a sampling of the employees who work in your organization. For example, if this is relevant to your organization, you may want to be sure to include representatives from multiple departments, such as the human resource department, production departments, marketing department, accounts payable, and so forth. While these individuals may only participate in a portion of the overall organization, their work matters, their voice matters, and their ownership in developing the mission matters.

In addition to gathering a contingent of individuals inside the organization, you may think to include those outside the organization. Capturing the voice of the customer or those served by the organization can lead to some very key insights as to the perception or value of your organization. In capturing that voice, you may find that the value you provide to others needs to be concretized in your why statement.

When developing your purpose—that is, creating your why—capturing the voices of those impacted by the organization allows those people inside the organization to gather vital information and provide input into the purpose of the organization. Allowing your people to hear from others as to the value you provide allows them, in turn, to define and capture the *why* of the organization.

As a leader, creating this type of environment for employees will support and foster their sense of ownership. **Ownership breeds engagement and giving people voice fosters ownership.** There is a lot of power in informing your people from the outside, expanding their perspective, and then putting them to work defining the why of your existence. You may be amazed at how people change when they feel heard and listened to in a genuine manner. Not just lip service. Fostering this type of environment in an organization leads to much deeper engagement. And while developing the why of your organization is not the only way to engage employees it is a solid first step in getting people involved.

Question Your Way to *Why*: The Voice of Your Employees

Capturing your organizational purpose with groups inside the organization, requires preparation and planning. To approach this work, leaders need to come to the table prepared to intently listen to answers to simple foundational questions. After gathering data there needs to be a time to review, synthesize, and create a collective purpose for your organization. Let us start with some foundational questions. (Note: This list of questions is not meant to be exhaustive. These questions are meant to prompt thinking; therefore you may find there are some other prompts more specific to the nuance of your work that may need to be asked as well.)

When we are digging into the purpose of our organization, we are asking foundational questions that will open up dialogue leading to the who, what, how, and why of our organizational existence.

Getting to Your Purpose through the Voice of Your Employees
Who are we serving? Customers? Clients? Another business organization?
What service or product are we providing?
How is that product or service adding value to their lives? What are the benefits?
Why do we exist? What value are you adding to the world? What altruistic purpose do we have?

These are foundational questions allowing you to examine your work and extract your purpose. Going back to NASA's purpose:

(NASA) purpose: *As explores, pioneers, and innovators, we boldly expand frontiers in air and space to inspire and serve America and to benefit the quality of life on Earth.* It answers these very basic questions and gives those that work for NASA a very clear picture as to why they exist.

NASA answers the question of *who* they are we serving very clearly. They are serving America. NASA serves the American people by being innovators and explorers. They provide awe inspiring information and photography that baffles our minds, leads us to question all we know, and give us a picture into the cosmos. Their work is awe inspiring and that is *what* they do to serve the American people. They answer their *how* by stating that they *inspire and serve* America. NASA adds value to people's lives by inspiring them through their work and they leave many people in awe and wonder. NASA completes their mission statement by expression how they add value to the world by stating that they seek to benefit the quality of life on earth. They work to make human existence better and when they frame their mission statement as this, they are not just working to gather photography, seek new frontiers, or engineering amazing machines, they are working for the betterment of humankind. This is a *why* that people can get behind, put in their hearts and work toward.

Southwest Airlines answers the same basic questions in their mission statement as well: *The mission of Southwest Airlines is dedication to the highest quality of customer service delivered with a sense of warmth, friendliness, individual pride, and company spirit.*

They approach their statement with a focus on the who and what. They are seeking to provide the highest quality customer services to those who fly their airlines. How do they provide that service? Through a sense of warmth, friendliness, individual pride, and company spirit. And although they may not explicitly describe the value they are an addition to the world they do explicitly say that they are dedicated to customer service. In other words, they are dedicated to serving people and there is nothing more noble.

Question Your Way to *Why*: The Voice of Your Customers

Much like capturing the voice of our internal employees, we must also consider the voice of our customers. In using the word *customer*, I am referring more generically to those your organization may serve or for whom they provide a product. The word *customer* is not intended to speak to only those in the business world but to be a more overarching term used for those your organization is purposed. We can also substitute customer for other stakeholders as necessary. You get the drift.

When gathering input from your customers or outside stakeholders, you will again want to come prepared with a set of question prompts that capture what you mean to your customers or those you serve:

Getting to Your Purpose through the Voice of Your Customer
What service or product are we providing to you?
Why do you choose our product or service over that of our competition?
How does our product or service add value to your life? What are the benefits of our service or product?
How can we improve your customer experience? What suggestions do you have for improvement?
Would you recommend our product or service to someone else? Why or why not?

(Note: Again, this list of questions is not meant to be exhaustive. These questions are meant to prompt thinking; therefore you may find there are some other prompts more specific to the nuance of your work that may need to be asked as well.)

As we set the stage to develop the *why* of our organization, it is necessary that we gather input from various stakeholders and ask some very foundational questions. In doing so, we have to set the table for these meetings and discussions with genuine honesty, trust, and thoughtfulness. Creating the right social and emotional environment for any meeting requires us to be careful about how we set the stage for building a community of people who are dedicated to developing the very important *why* of the organization.

Setting the Table for Genuine Conversations

I recently attended a dinner meeting that included several leaders within the organization I was working with. When we came together, there was a clear purpose for our meeting, and our time together was set aside to be meaningful for all of us. When we decided on where to meet, we found it important that the environment of the meeting align with our purpose for the meeting. Our dinner included a well-set table, nice food, and the right ambiance for us. It was an environment that allowed us to have the close conversations and dialogue about meaningful and purposeful topics.

I describe this because as you sit down with your people and seek to create the *why* of your organization it is important that you set the table for your people. Creating the right physical and social-emotional environment allows people to come to the table with a sense of trust and openness for a genuine dialogue. [31]Peter Block, in his book *Community: The Structure of Belonging*, shares the importance of creating the right meeting environment that will allow for a true sense of trust, community and belonging. If we expect to have true and honest dialogue in any meeting, the right environment must be set. Block goes as far as to state that we have to be thoughtful about the room, the layout, lighting, and the location. We have to be thoughtful about how people are arranged. Is it auditorium seating, small group seating, or is it a boardroom? The point here is this: When you are setting the table to work with any group of people for any prospective outcome, as leaders who seeks to engage people, we must make sure the table is set, the environment is right, we know why we are meeting, and we build deep-seated trust and community. Being highly intentional about creating the right environment will allow for more thoughtful, open, trusting, and productive conversations that will get you and your organization to the center of your *why*.

Design Tools for Capturing Voices

To summarize briefly, let me share: Ray Dalio, one of the most successful hedge fund managers of our time and author of *Principles*,

---

[31]Peter Block, *Community: The Structure of Belonging* (Oakland, CA: Berrett-Koehler Publishers, 2018).

shares this: "I believe that all organizations basically have two types of people: those who work to be part of a mission, and those who work for a paycheck."[32] Our efforts are focused on designing an environment for our people that fosters support for our mission, our *why*. When we seek to engage our employees in the mission and purpose, we make genuine efforts to capture their voices, solicit their input and give them a platform to share their ideas. To do so, we can design a set of simple prompts or questions that lead us to collective thinking around the why of our existence. Generally speaking, we simply ask: What we are doing? How are we doing it? Why are we doing it? What does it do to support others? And while we steep ourselves in this work, we need to ensure we set the table, creating the climate that allows for genuine, trust-filled communications.

Once that stage is set, we are able to capture genuine input, data, ideas, and information through several optional tools. When collecting voices, we can utilize a multitude of tools that may include surveys, focus groups, brainstorming, and affinity diagramming, just to name a few. How we chose to capture those voices relies heavily on the product or service with which we are involved. These tools allow businesses and organizations to capture stakeholder voices and data, that when synthesized, can lead an organization to their collective mission and purpose:

Surveys

When we are capturing the voice of our internal and external stakeholders, surveys serve as very useful tools in capturing large amounts of data in a relatively efficient manner. Surveys can be designed to be gather information electronically allowing for efficient sorting and analysis. Further, surveys allow for the asking of simple "yes" or "no" questions, one word answers, or questions that require a short or long response. In working with one large urban school district in the state of Illinois we sought to gather data from over twenty-five hundred employees as to the nature of their engagement and their finding purpose in their work. We were able to push out the survey through the organizational email and quickly capture the voice of close to 90 percent of our employees. Our data,

---

[32]Ray Dalio, *Principles: Life and Work* (New York: Simon and Schuster, 2017).

after analysis, allowed us to better focus our mission and define our future goals for the district, its students, our employees, and our community. Surveys can be a very pragmatic way to capture both the voice of your employees and your customers, and they allow you to ask questions that will get you to the heart of your *why*.

Focus Groups

Capturing internal and external voices can also be done through thoughtful and careful focus groups. Working with individual stakeholder groups can allow for the free flow of thoughtful answers to well-planned questions, and it can also lead to new questions and new answers. When conducting focus groups discussions, it is important to come to the table well prepared with questions that lead to your purpose and also allow for enough flexibility to allow the conversation to open up to new insights for which you may not be aware.

When writing my doctoral dissertation, I conducted focus group work while doing preliminary research. When I came to the table, I was prepared with specific questions related to the nature of employee engagement within the organization I was working with at that time. While my questions were precise and clearly directed to lead us in the right direction, the responses to some of my questions opened up new doors and insights. Again, while I came with questions, I remained open enough to gain insights, which were appreciated, thoughtful, and led to new understanding.

Focus groups can be remarkably telling and can lead to great information gathering. I would like to add here just a few simple tips that may help when running a focus group. First, as mentioned before, set the table. Create an environment in which people can speak freely, openly, and with genuine professionalism. As a leader, part of your role to create this type of environment. Second, I recommend transparently videotaping or recording the conversation. Capturing the data from focus groups is challenging and having video or audio to go back to will allow you to better capture all comments, conversational themes, responses, and potentially, nonverbal reactions. Finally, I recommend allowing for a post focus group survey. Essentially, asking the same or similar questions to the group in a short-answer electronic survey format to gather any new information, alternate ideas, or any other information that may not have come out due to the dynamics of the focus group.

Brainstorming

Beyond surveys and focus groups, as you work your way toward a deeper and shared understanding of your organizational *why*, it may be important to brainstorm informally or formally with other members associated with your organization. Gathering the voice of your people and your customers through brainstorming sessions can also lead to some valuable insight. Gathering people from your leadership teams, executive boards, or across departments may allow for some viewpoints that may not have been shared in other groups.

In one school district I worked with, I chaired a fairly large committee of about fifteen district-wide employees who all shared similar job responsibilities. Although their roles were important, they served as support roles to regular classroom teachers and students and may not have had a voice in the organization outside this committee. However, in my meetings with this committee, I would often seek information through brainstorming and find little nuggets of truth that I may have not found working with other groups. Their view of our work and their perspectives proved to be very enlightening and led to great improvements within our organization. Point being, seeking out additional voices and conducting brainstorming sessions can lead to some new insights that will potentially lead you to the heart of your why.

Affinity Mapping and Theming

After gathering voices from both inside and outside the organization, you will be left with plenty of data and ideas that will lead you to your *why* statement. Organizing, sorting, and theming the data will require you and your team to take some time to unpack all that you have gathered from your surveys, focus groups, and/or brainstorming sessions. In doing so, your team will need begin theming—that is, creating a picture of common statements and ideas that have been gathered from the voices of your people.

One way to theme is through affinity mapping. Affinity mapping simply requires your team to capture similar ideas and put them into categories. For example, your team may be unpacking the data that was gathered from a survey or focus group around the question: *Why do you choose your product or service over that of the competition*? While theming that question, you will want to give each person on your team a pad of Post-it notes and have them begin writing down common language that they see throughout the survey or focus group responses. As each person writes down common words or phrases to the questions have them come stick the Post-it notes up on a board where they can be housed until everyone is done. After that is complete, and you have a lot of Post-it notes on your board, create a foursquare and begin to categorize the statements into themes. With all the responses, you may find that there are some similar themes such as quality, convenience, customer service, or others. Creating these themes and categorizing responses will allow you to get a clearer and more concise picture of the responses you have gathered. And while this is a simple example, and not intended to be a technical manual on theming, I hope you get the picture here. As you gather data with your team, it is important that you unpack this information to get a collective aerial perspective of the common responses in order to better craft a purpose statement that gives voice to the people inside and outside the organization.

Communication Plan—Communicating Your Why

Developing and crafting your purpose as a team or organization is certainly a very valuable exercise in engaging your people and giving them voice and ownership in their work. It doesn't end with the writing of your why statement, however. From this point, your mission statement must be adopted, published, and lived daily through a solid communication plan. It is not enough to craft a why statement. You must have it become part of your brand, and it must become commonplace in your organization. If you expect your employees to own the *why* of the organization, it must become habitually spoken, visually ubiquitous, and culturally practiced. Making your why statement a part of everyday life, belief and practice takes intentionality. Here are a few things to consider when adopting a why statement:

- Branding: A why statement should be communicated regularly through organizational branding such as the organization's website, newsletters, quarterly reports, and the like. Additionally, all internal letterhead, agendas. And communications should include your *why*.

- Meetings: All meetings should include the why of your organization. Whether meetings are large or small, the organizational why should be communicated and reviewed. Being consistent and clear in your why reminds everyone in the organization why they are here and why they and their work are so important.

- Reflection and review cycles: All organizations, teams, families, business, etc., should include regular reflection and review cycles. These are times when you reflect upon your goals, objectives, and progress. It is during these times when your why should receive extraspecial attention and promotion. All members within the organization should be reminded of the foundational mission of their work and its purpose.

- Serves as a filter: Your why statement, while it drives your purpose, should also serve as a filter for sifting out organizational activities that are not aligned with your purpose. Too often organizations lose focus and move in tangential directions. Your why statement should be communicated regularly to keep your organization on track and focused while eliminating distractions.

Throughout my career, I have gone through the process of developing many why statements. I have been the leader of teams and also played supporting roles. What I have found is that the ingredients that make this process a success are clear, open, genuine communication among people and leaders; and a solid communication plan that allows the *why* of your organization to become ingrained in the everyday beliefs, routines, habits, and rituals. Your why should not just be a statement on a poster hung in the boardroom. Your *why* statement should be the reason your organization has life. It should be known by everyone in the organization, and it should serve to communicate the reason your organization exists.

Summary

Creating an environment in which people are engaged, where people find meaning and purpose in their work, is a truly beautiful act of care and love. When we lead others from a place of personal completeness and seek to promote the well-being and contentment of others, we are leading with love. As leaders who care to create engaging and meaningful work environments, let us not forget the elements that prove to motivate people. People are motivated and more apt to engage in their work when given an opportunity for meaning and purpose in their work.[33] Involving your people in the development of your organizational purpose allows each person a voice to speak to the meaning and impact of the organization in which they are involved.

While you work with your team to develop a collective purpose, recognize the intent of this exercise. Developing a collective purpose allows for your people to engage in the design of your organization's *why*. It allows your people to take ownership and commit to the mission of the organization and involving multiple voices creates an environment in which people are heard and included.

After setting the table, gathering data, and framing the exercise as a purposeful and meaningful endeavor, it's time to create your why. This can be tedious and may involve several iterations but essentially your team has to work together to create a why that captures the genuine benefits of your work. Your team is charged with creating a statement that tells people inside and outside the organization why you exist and what value you bring to the lives of others. Just as NASA seeks to "expand frontiers in air and space to inspire and serve America and to benefit the quality of life on Earth," your team is responsible for sharing with the world how you will make the lives of other people better. How will you and your team add value to the human experience and the lives of people?

---

[33]Deci, Edward L., and Richard M. Ryan. "Self-determination theory." (2012).

Love in Action

- Why is employee engagement important to your organization? Why is creating an environment in which employees have a sense of purpose and ownership beneficial to the work of your organization?

- Does your organization have a *why* statement? Whose voice needs to be included in the development of your why?

  - Develop a focus group strategy that includes both internal and external voices and begin developing the why of your organization.

- Do the employees within your organization know the value of their work and what they are doing to improve the lives of others?

  - Survey employees and members within the organization to get an understanding of the value they attach to their work. Ask employees if their work serves to improve the lives of others.

- When you set the table for your why, who needs to be included? What tools will you use to devise your statement? How will you communicate your plan and make it part of everyday life in your organization?

  - Be intentional about how you plan. Be organized, detailed, and succinct. As you move through the development of your organizational *why*, be sure to be well planned in every facet of its creation and communication.

Chapter

Engagement through Teaming

*Nothing drives strong teams like great performance, and what
drives strong performance is a commitment to a shared vision,
shared goals with behaviors and relationships aligned with
reaching those goals.*

—Dr. Henry Cloud

One of the most rewarding, beautiful, and exciting elements of
leadership is building strong teams. The strength of a team often
serves to be a measuring stick for their effectiveness. When teams
are focused, organized, and function as well-driven systems, they
can produce incredible outcomes. In chapter 6, we will look at
how developing strong teams improves the engagement of people,
drives social connections, and gives team members opportunities to
contribute in meaningful and powerful ways.

We have looked at the importance of engaging our people in developing
our organizational *why*. Doing so, drives your organization's

purpose and motivates people to be driven toward meaningful work. As leaders who intend to lead from a place of love, engaging people through the development of the organizational *why* allows for people to be connected to their work in a social and emotional manner. **It is our duty as leaders to create opportunities and environments that give people meaning and purpose, not only for their sake but also because when we design engaging environments we are ready and able to fulfill our goals as an organization**. In addition to engaging your people in the development of the organizational *why*, creating a collaborative, team-based environment serves to engage people in their work through strong relational connections, decreased social isolation, and a shared mission and purpose.

A colleague of mine took over the reins of a large suburban high school outside Chicago in the early 2000s. This school had a reputation for success and for the most part was operating well. For him, doing things well was not good enough. So, in order to move his team from good to great, he implemented a team-based strategy that got people collaborating, sharing ideas, and working together in one direction. Schools, much like business, include various departments, committees, and teams that serve the larger goal of the organization. Ensuring that those departments are operating effectively requires intentional effort in developing team cohesiveness. Teams rarely gel without having some intentional structure, rituals, and/or routines.

My colleague, knowing that he had to move his teams in the right direction, made some very commonsense shifts in the way teams, departments, and committees operated. He began by ensuring that teams were given the time to meet on a regular basis with goals and objectives for their meetings. Additionally, he coached teams in the development and operation of regular routines, habits, and decision-making strategies.[34] In creating a team-based, organization, he tapped into the motivators of autonomy, ownership, and mastery,[35] which I will discuss further in this chapter. He also sought to understand the strengths and weaknesses of his team members in

[34]Charles Duhigg, *The Power of Habit: Why We Do What We Do in Life and Business* (New York: Random House, 2012).
[35]Daniel H. Pink, *Drive: The Surprising Truth About What Motivates Us* (New York: Penguin Press, 2011).

order to maximize individual strengths and hedge against individual weaknesses.

Developing strong teams who are aligned to the mission, purpose, and *why* of the organization creates an atmosphere that fosters effectiveness, creativity, and drive. The research is clear on this subject. When we create team environments that support collaboration, autonomy, and ownership, we set the stage for success while creating fulfillment and meaning in the lives of our people.

It's Not Just a Paycheck

I recently had a conversation with a graduate student who was attending Harvard Business School. In our conversation, I was asking her how she was managing her work life as well as her personal and academic life. With such a demanding schedule I was curious as to how she was getting along. Her response was really quite refreshing. She explained that she loved what she was doing both at work and at Harvard and she was integrating a life that included her personal and professional goals. We often hear people refer to work-life balance, which supposes that work and life are two separate entities that live and operate in isolation of one another. Her response, however, captures the notion of work-life integration. This is where people experience purposeful work that aligns with their mission and enjoyment of life. The beauty of work-life integration is that it encapsulates the idea that we can find enjoyment and fulfillment in our work and that our work is equally as important to a meaningful life as our personal time.

A few years back, a close family friend was explaining to me that he "worked to live, not live to work." What he meant by that was that his work added little value to his life other than a paycheck. He did not enjoy the way he spent a third of his day, it was solely for sustenance. What he really wanted was to get home from work and enjoy the rest of his day outside the world of work. This is a sad state in which to live and seems to me to be a waste of a large portion of the purpose of our lives. As leaders of our homes, community organizations, or businesses, it is our role to support the establishment of an environment that leads to work-life integration and not a work-life separation.

John Maxwell, author of the *Five Levels of Leadership*,[36] tells a humorous story about how those who are largely disengaged in their work and care little about the organization will pull their cars in backward to their parking spots in order to speed out as quickly as possible to maximize their personal time. He shares that those who don't like their work will look at the clock with ten minutes before the end of the day and choose to go to the bathroom because they need to pee on company time rather than waste their own! Why waste their own time to pee after work when they can do it on company time, he explains! I find it humorous, but I know it is true. I have seen and worked in organizations where the leadership takes little interest in engaging people in their work and as a result people pull their cars in backward and make sure to pee on company time.

You know what I am talking about. You have seen or maybe even worked with organizations that don't tap into people's motivations and do little to create a healthy work environment—leaders who care little about others but seek to make themselves look good or improve their own financial situation. Maybe you have seen an organization that is so overly bureaucratic it removes the human element from the equation. People feel there is no connection to the work or the organization. Or worse yet, the disengaged leader who has been handed the reins only to create an environment of compliance. Having worked with schools and businesses for over two decades I have unfortunately seen these types of leaders and these types of environments too often, and it leads to disengagement and a lack of employee satisfaction and motivation.

For our purposes and for those of us who intend to lead from a place of love, it is necessary to tap into people's motivations and seek to set up environments that tap into people's willingness to share their lives with us and our organization. Sure, we could set up an authoritative system that demands compliance, but in doing so you will not bring people's hearts, minds, or motivations into their work. As leaders who seek the love of leadership, we want to lead people by capturing their motivations. We want to engage people in their work for their fulfillment and the health of the organization.

[36] John C. Maxwell, *The 5 Levels of Leadership: Proven Steps to Maximize Your Potential* (New York: Center Street, 2011).

It Is a Social Exchange

I have a dear friend and a colleague who has worked in upper management for an international manufacturing company for several years. He has had many roles within the organization, and he has done very well in helping lead the organization to success. His heart, however, had not been in it, and he recently decided to make a change that left him finding work that gave him greater meaning, motivation, and purpose. While working for the manufacturing company, he was subject to implementing a management strategy that demanded long hours, little human empathy, and the denial of individualism. And while leaders want their employees to give of themselves for the organization it is important to understand that in our modern, democratic culture, people make a choice to give of themselves and want something more than a paycheck in return. Trying to force people into organizational compliance and giving little in return other than a paycheck will often lead to minimal motivation and buy in. Understanding that people exchange their time and their will for what motivates and drives them allows us to set the stage for an engaging work environment. With that, my friend made a change to choose to work with an organization that values people, their time, and their engagement. This new organization seeks to motivate by offering a work environment that supports people's hearts, minds, and motivations—and yes, a paycheck—in exchange for each individual's hard work and drive.

Sociologists and psychologists refer to this as a social exchange. People are willing to give of themselves for something in return. Take volunteerism for example, people are willing to give up their time and resources, not for a paycheck, but for what? People exchange their time and resources for a purpose and for a cause bigger than themselves. They seek to serve others because they know in their hearts they were made to do so. They give of their time and energy not to receive a monetary reward but to receive a reward of the heart. People are willing to give of themselves for others to find more fulfillment in their lives. Prosocial endeavors such as volunteering leads people to exchange their time and energy for feelings of good will and service to others.

The role of the leader is to understand that this social exchange exists and then to create the right social and emotional climate for people to want to come to work and give of their time, hearts, minds, and motivations. Yes, work creates a monetary exchange, which I do not want to diminish, but capturing people's hearts is equally important. People need to know that they are doing work for the service of the greater good whether it's working for NASA, in schools, in retail, or in manufacturing. They need to feel a sense of connection to the people in the organization and feel that they are a part of a team. Supporting people through strong teaming leads to a stronger sense of social exchange. The military, for example, is known for creating such social dynamics. Many veterans when returning to the civilian world will express a loss of connection or community with their fellow military men and women. Many who enlist in the military share their sense of connection to their brothers and sisters as being one of the greatest elements of their service. Similar to the military, creating a close and connected community within your organization, department, or committees will lead your staff to a more deeply engaging and fulfilling work environment for which individuals are willing to give of themselves.

Team Motivations: AMP

Before mapping out some of the strategies for quality team development, it is important to understand the key elements of human motivation, which serve as the foundation of good teaming. People and organizations thrive when a certain motivational recipe supports the social exchange we just mentioned above. In order to create strong, collaborative, and engaging team environments, teams need to be able to have a sense of autonomy, mastery, and purpose. I refer to this as AMPs. Much like our electronic devices rely on the amps of electricity to run, so too do our staff and our teams rely on AMPs to drive and move forward. Ensuring that your teams are offered opportunities for autonomy in their work, mastery in their craft, and purpose in their efforts, will serve to create a more engaging work environment in which your people will be more apt to give of themselves for the purpose and mission.

Autonomy

When creating engaging team environments autonomy is a key ingredient. I am not talking about people being completely independent of the organization, I am referring to giving teams opportunities to have autonomous actions that support the purpose of the organization as a whole. This may include having teams design specific processes and protocols that support the mission of the department or organization.

One quick example includes my working with a human resources department. The goal of the department was to hire high-quality employees who could connect to a social environment, embody core competencies of the job, and add value to the organization. With that said, when I conferred with the department we found there to be a high turnover rate and people who were hired were not matching the core competency expectations. The Human Resources department was then asked to make some autonomous decisions. They were asked to reflect on their hiring practices, examine the human capital development plan, and make recommendations for a change plan that would address these issues. The human resources team was given the autonomy to examine the areas of needed improvement, make recommendations, and develop a plan to improve the human resources department.

The recommendations the team came up with were discussed and examined as a team. Many of the change recommendations were implemented and stress tested. Some of the changes the HR team made became permanent while others were reexamined, changed and adjusted over time. The point here is this: The HR team was involved in the improvement process. They were given a voice and an opportunity to impact one of the most important processes in the organization. They were not handed a new process from an outside consultant, rather, they were asked to dig in, make recommendations and in turn they took ownership in improving the organization. **Giving people autonomy to use their skill and their will motivates people and engages them in meaningful work.**

Mastery

Another driving force that motivates people is an individual's will to do things well and master their craft. People are driven to make their mark and they are driven toward improvements. Giving your staff an opportunity to master their work, make improvements, and make meaningful contributions captures individual self-determination and serves as another component of human motivation. People have a driving force to take ownership of their lives and allowing them opportunities to determine their outcomes, express their individual creativity, or express ideas, lends to the motivational recipe.

In the late 2000s, I brought together a project management team who had far more experience in their field than I had. I was simply looking at their processes from the outside while they knew the inner workings of their business well. The team was unable to coordinate their efforts and regularly had process redundancies and gaps. In my working with this group my role was to lead them to visualizing and understanding their process errors and then allow them to brainstorm, and process map their way to an improvement plan.

The team was given an opportunity to master this process and create corrective steps to ensure their effectiveness. The team worked together to identify their gaps in communication and processes and developed a tool that would ensure each team member was completing their portion of the task. This shared collaborative tool served to create a process that allowed each team member to see where the others were in the overall process sequence, which allowed each member to operate on real-time information. The process tool the team created also gave team members a sense of individual mastery, where they were able to visualize their process completion and share that completion with the overall team. The members of the team shared how much they enjoyed being able to mark their completion of a task and the little dose of accomplishment that it gave them.

This team was given an opportunity to improve their work process by offering them the time to master their work environment. Allowing teams the opportunity to work together to engage in the improvement process gives each team member greater buy-in into their work and creates a system that supports their team environment and their shared purpose and responsibilities. When we want people to engage in their work, we need to give them the chance to impact their work. Fostering opportunities for them to master their work supports greater engagement.

Purpose

While working with teams to foster a more engaging work environment, creating a sense of purpose and tapping into their *why* are essential. And while I believe we have covered the importance of a purpose both personally and professionally, I would like to share a quick example of the power of team purpose.

Several years ago, I had the privilege of working with a team of teachers who represented a district's dual-language program. When I began my work with this team, their program lacked organization, purpose, and was only loosely defined. The program lacked objectives or measurable outcomes and it was not in line with best educational practices. As I began working closely with this team, I quickly realized two things: 1) In the past, the members were not given a voice to impact the decisions around the program; and 2) the program lacked a purpose. For example, questions such as the following had not been asked: Why did this program exist? Who was it designed to serve? How would it serve them? What benefits did it offer to students?

As I worked closely with the team, we intentionally established the purpose of the program with the voice of every teacher represented on the team. The process was real, it was genuine, and it created a real love for and buy-in into the dual language program. The end product of this specific task was a program that defined its *why,* and a program description that outlined the goals, objectives, and outcomes of the program. The point here is this: The collective efforts of the team created a strong sense of engagement and buy-in into the program by establishing a purpose for their program. This work matched their values, goals, and objectives. This symbiotic relationship between the team and its purpose created a deeper sense of engagement for this group of teachers, and it led to a far more effective program.

Establishing the Rules of Engagement

Creating an engaged and effective team requires intentionality, and there may be a few trials in getting there, but the creation of a strong team can lead to a beautiful system that supports meaningful work and meaningful relationships. When teams are well established with the intentional rules of engagement, they allow people to be genuinely open to ideas, feedback, and organizational improvement. **Strong teams that work together with integrity, openness, and drive do not happen by accident. Rather, they grow and develop through honest and genuine conversation and relationship building around the rules of engagement.** Conversations that define those rules are critical and play a foundational role in team development. This includes asking the pointed questions that lead to established rules and norms of behavior.

When

Beyond knowing the desired outcomes of the team, when a team begins working together they must establish a regular and consistent *when*. The team must decide how often they will meet and for how long. When a team has decided on clear expectations for regular meetings and the length of those meetings, they are intentionally establishing regular space and time to focus on specific tasks. The *when* element of team building is critical for establishing consistency in relationship building and workflow. It also allows for the regular progress monitoring of goals and objectives and supports regular review of the team's processes and outcomes. When teams meet on an irregular basis, with unclear expectations, it promotes inconsistent workflow, lack of clarity, and weak outcomes.

Communication Rules

Establishing behavioral rules related to communication is also critical to a team. Discussing how the team will listen, communicate, and prevent disruptions allows teams to communicate with greater ease and clarity. Examples of clarifying questions may be: How will we listen? How will we handle interruptions? How will we move from one communicator to the next? How do we ensure all have a voice? How do we ensure all participate? Establishing such rules gives each member clear expectations for how to communicate and respect the other members of the team. It also allows each person a platform to provide input. Communication rules set the stage for open communications that capture the voice of each of the participants within the team.

Building Consensus

Establishing rules for decision-making is also critical in molding sound and effective team decisions. In creating an environment for building consensus, there are two key elements to consider: 1) the decision-making process—that is, how you will come to consensus; and 2) transparent merits of each team member. As leaders, when it comes time to make critical decisions and solve problems we must have a systematic process for dealing with decision-making while also knowing the capacities of the individuals on your team. In doing so, we want to capture the most knowledgeable voices on the team to inform and provide input in order for us to make the best possible decisions. Very simply, let's use the US president's cabinet as an example: The president will often put specific cabinet members around him who offer him specific information related to their expertise. Conversations may include nonexperts on the topic, but at the end of the day the president makes decisions with the input of the most trusted advisor in that specific area.

In our own organizations, it is also necessary to establish systems for decision-making. Doing so supports a stable and consistent environment for those individuals on the team and allows them to understand the overall rules of engagement. The use of a democratic decision-making processes, in conjunction with the use of specific decision-making protocols, allows people to provide input while getting to the point of consensus. Let me share an example: In the early 2000s, I worked with the leadership team of a Fortune 500 company. Once a week we conducted sales meetings where we unpacked our sales data, charted our progress, and sought new ways to reach our goals. As we shared our data, we sought the advice and experience of the most successful members of the sales team to help drive our decision-making process. These individuals had stood the test of time and had the experience, knowledge, and proven track record to help us reach our goals. The meetings were tight, well run, and when we got to the point of making decisions we had solid input from all voices with an emphasis on our most trusted salespeople.

Allowing us to gather sound information from our salespeople then led us to sharing our ideas and making decisions by utilizing a set of meeting protocols. We used a simple protocol—that is, a set of questions, that we created to assist us down a path to improved decision-making. This protocol worked for our sales team and can be augmented to improve decision-making processes in many other arenas. See the example (figure 6.1).

6.1 Example: Making Decisions and Problem-Solving Protocol

Questions	Explanation
What is our sales data showing us?	We started with sales data to be able to appropriately identify our strengths and our areas for growth.
What areas of strength require our attention?	We asked this question to ensure we were capitalizing on our strengths and not succumb to solely focusing on our areas of weakness.
What area of growth can we capitalize on?	We asked this question to be able to discuss what we could reasonably improve upon that was within our control?
What are the internal and external root causes of our areas of growth?	We asked this question to get to the truth of the matter and be able to understand the current reality. This was critical and often challenging. This conversation required genuine trust, openness, and transparency.
Who has expertise in this area that can support our understanding of the problem or challenge?	This question served to capture the voice of our experts on the sales team.
What are our proposed solutions?	We would often gather several ideas as to how to impact our growth areas and post them for all of us to see.
Merit-based decision-making and point system voting.	Based on the data and well experienced voices we would discuss our proposed solutions. We would examine the pros and cons. If there was no clear consensus, we would assign a point value (1–5) to each solution, 5 being strong support and 1 being weak support. We would look to use the point system to drive consensus.

The protocol we use is just one simple example of a systems approach to decision-making that captures the voices of the team. People and teams thrive when there are rules that provide structure and engage members. The example above shows how the team had a system for decision-making while relying on the merits of the members. There are numerous protocols that can support team decision-making, the one I shared here is just one example that was successful in one arena. **Knowing your business and your people will require systematic thinking to create a structure and system that works for your team.** I will share additional examples in part III.

Know Who Is on the Team

When developing engaging team environments in which people thrive and find meaning in their work it is necessary to know who is on your team in order to be able to understand their ways of thinking, feeling, and working. Strong team dynamics does not happen by accident and requires an analysis of the team members to ensure team cohesion. One way to do this is to capitalize on the use of personality tests such as the Myers-Briggs Type Indicator ®. The Myers-Briggs allows for a deeper understanding of personality types and uncovers individual ways of thinking and behaving. Like any personality test, there is a margin of error, but taking the MBTI as a team and sharing the results with one another supports conversations that create a clearer understanding of who is at the table and their ways of thinking and behaving. Below is a synopsis of the Myers-Briggs.[37]

Myers-Briggs theory is an adaptation of the theory of psychological types produced by Carl Gustav Jung. It is based on 16 personality types, which Jung viewed as stereotypes (Jung 1921, p. 405). They act as useful reference points to understand your unique personality (Jung 1957, p. 304). At the heart of Myers Briggs theory are four preferences. Do you prefer to deal with:

• People and things (Extraversion or "E"), or ideas and information (Introversion or "I").

• Facts and reality (Sensing or "S"), or possibilities and potential (Intuition or "N").

• Logic and truth (Thinking or "T"), or values and relationships (Feeling or "F").

[37]https://www.teamtechnology.co.uk/tt/t-articl/mb-simpl.htm

- A lifestyle that is well-structured (Judgment or "J"), or one that goes with the flow (Perception or "P").

In Myers Briggs theory, for each pair, you prefer one style more than the other. Jung also allowed a middle group, where you like an equal balance of the two. You combine the letters associated with your preferences to get your Myers Briggs personality type. For example, having preferences for E, S, T, and J gives a personality type of ESTJ. Although you have preferences, you still use all eight styles—in the same way that most people are right-handed, but they still use both hands.

Extraversion and Introversion—The first pair of styles is concerned with the direction of your energy. If you prefer to direct your energy to deal with people, things, situations, or "the outer world," then your preference is for Extraversion. If you prefer to direct your energy to deal with ideas, informatwion, explanations, or beliefs, or "the inner world," then your preference is for Introversion.

Sensing and Intuition—The second pair concerns the type of information and things that you process. If you prefer to deal with facts, what you know, to have clarity, or to describe what you see, then your preference is for Sensing. If you prefer to deal with ideas, look into the unknown, to generate new possibilities or to anticipate what isn't obvious, then your preference is for Intuition. The letter N is used for intuition because I has already been allocated to introversion.

Thinking and Feeling—The third pair reflects your style of decision-making. If you prefer to decide on the basis of objective logic, using an analytic and detached approach, then your preference is for thinking. If you prefer to decide using values—that is, on the basis of what or who you believe is important—then your preference is for feeling.

Judgment and Perception—The final pair describes the type of lifestyle you adopt. If you prefer your life to be planned and well-structured, then your preference is for judging. This is not to be confused with "judgmental,' which is quite different. If you prefer to go with the flow, to maintain flexibility, and respond to things as they arise, then your preference is for Perception.

https://www.teamtechnology.co.uk/tt/t-articl/mb-simpl.htm

While the Myers-Briggs is an often-used personality test, I would also recommend the Enneagram test. The Enneagram test also allows for a deeper look into individual personalities, emotional dispositions, and behavioral types. Both the MBTI and the Enneagram Test can be used to unpack understandings of the individuals on the team and can lead to some very open and honest conversations about who sits around the team table and the state of their minds, emotions, and behaviors.

Knowing who is at the table allows for a more genuine understanding of viewpoints, truth, and transparency. When we can understand more deeply the personalities and propensities of our team members, we are positioned for more honest and genuine interactions among members. Teams that display strong cohesion are marked with a sense of connection, understanding and transparency. Getting to that point, however, requires teams to take explicit and intentional steps in getting to know one another and being open to others' dispositions.

Getting to genuinely know one another is not always easy and does require strong leadership, transparency, and an immense level of trust. When achieved, however, teams who know each other use their individual strengths to uncover truths, solve problems, and capture reality. Knowing each other gives team members an opportunity to see blind spots in one another's thinking and openly share ideas. These blind spots in thinking and problem-solving are often left out of sight when team members are unable to share in truth and honesty. But when team members are aware of the individual strengths and merits of each member, they are better able to shed light on blind spots, gaps in thinking, limited understanding, and biases. When team members can share openly and honestly while being understood by the other individuals on the team for their perspectives and merits, we create an environment that thrives and leads to effective critical thinking and problem-solving.

Trust and Transparency

Achieving high levels of trust and transparency is difficult and requires teams to act with genuine openness, honesty, kindness, and love. High levels of trust and transparency requires immense integrity and truthfulness. As leaders, it is our job to create the environment that supports these characteristics, and it is exceptionally important to model and embody such character strengths. Stephen Covey, in *the Speed of Trust*,[38] offers great insight into the importance of team trust and the rewards that high levels of trust offer. While it is important to trust the competences of our teammates it is also

---

[38]Stephen R. Covey and Rebecca R. Merrill, *The Speed of Trust: The One Thing That Changes Everything* (New York: Simon and Schuster, 2006).

important to trust their character. Team environments in which trust is strong include high levels of openness and honesty. We develop trust in one another when we know that we are able to be clear on our input and share our thoughts and ideas without negative emotional responses by other team members. **Meaning, that in order to establish trust people must be able to share their ideas in an environment that offers critical feedback but does not demean individual personhood. When the sharing of ideas is met with emotional criticism or backroom conversations, trust is diminished, and team members will not bring their best to the team. Trust requires genuine openness and can be easily lost if team members are not sharing with a sense of security.**

While trust requires openness, it also requires transparency—that is, members need to be able to show their hand, share their motivation, and know there is not a backroom agenda somewhere else. For example, if a team is working together to solve a problem, and the team makes a decision, only for that decision to later be overturned in a closed-door backroom conversation, trust will be lost. In order to maintain high levels of trust, the decisions have to be made openly with reason and rationale being understood by everyone. The notion that everyone has to agree is not the premise here. The notion here is that people need to be able to be transparent and share their ideas in a safe and collaborative work environment in order to gather sound input and make the best possible decisions with the highest levels of information from all participants.

While openness and transparency are easily said, they are not always easily achieved, and it is our job as leaders to embody the integrity necessary to model and support these behaviors. In doing so, we have to set the rules of engagement. It is our job to respect every voice and unpack the merits of ideas. We need to maintain integrity and avoid the backroom decision-making. We have to be upfront, honest, and transparent. We have to be crystal clear about the rules of engagement, use our protocols, and ensure our strength of character. We not only have to admit our mistakes and model that it is OK to be wrong, but we must also establish that it is not OK to gossip, it is not OK to disengage, and it is not OK to interrupt team cohesion. The strength of the team is of utmost importance, and when a strong team comes together it serves to benefit the goals and mission of the organization while also supporting each individual's sense of meaningfulness and personal fulfillment.

Rhythm of Consistency and Reciprocal Accountability

Great teams are often characterized by their ability to be in sync and to run fluently, effectively, and cohesively. They are often well versed and well practiced in their work and got there with heavy doses of intentionality and repetition. Great teams will also report a sense of teamwork and being accountable to one another. Meaning, they work for the betterment of the team and recognize in return what the team provides for them. Here I want to discuss two elements that support and foster strong teaming: rhythm of consistency and reciprocal accountability.

Rhythm of Consistency

Teams come together for the purpose of achieving specific goals, moving forward an initiative, or innovating new possibilities. In doing so, successful teams often act with a sense of rhythm in their work. They often develop a consistent system to achieve their goals that allow for continuity in their work. Developing a rhythm of consistency requires us as leaders to create the time and space for teams to approach their work together, on a regular basis, so as not to lose momentum or stymie progress.

Dr. Henry Cloud, in his book *Boundaries for Leaders*,[39] shares a story about a team who had been operating unsuccessfully but later turned the corner by establishing a rhythm of consistency. He shares that the team had been working in an environment in which individuals had unclear expectations and communication was severely lacking. Therefore, in order to overcome those challenges, they established a practice of regular Monday-morning meetings. Each Monday the team would come together, review their goals, and share their personal successes related to those goals. Team members would use their Monday-morning meeting to establish regular communication, maintain focus on the collective goal, and share best practices in their work.

---

[39]Cloud, Henry. *Boundaries for leaders*. Harper Audio, 2013.

In establishing this regular meeting routine, what this team had done was to create a continued focus that supported ongoing communication and understanding of best practices. Too often, teams lack consistency and don't recognize that putting in place simple routines can support team effectiveness. I have worked with educational leadership teams for over two decades and one of the simple differences between successful and unsuccessful teams is the ability to establish a simple rhythm that supports the regular focus on goals and outcomes.

In the 2010s, I worked closely with a high-level project management team that experienced the failure associated with lacking rhythm. They turned it around and later experienced success by simply establishing rhythm. The team had been working toward some very specific goals that required additional focus outside the scope of their normal focus and professional competencies. The project was largely related to a multimillion-dollar facility project that was not typical to their scope of work. The team felt bogged down by the heavy lifting of the project and the demands it was taking on their time. Their regular meetings were being dominated by this side project and it was taking away from their typical agenda. The team, not tending to their regular agenda, began to sputter and their effectiveness began to wane. After several months of slowed progress, it became apparent that the team needed to reestablish their focus on their core mission and thus created a separate time to tend to those items that were no longer being tended to through their regular leadership team meetings. While the team recognized that the facility project was placing significant demands on their time and disrupting their rhythm, they recognized the need for additional time to stay focused on their core mission. When they were disrupted, in order to remain effective, they reestablished a new rhythm elsewhere to continue their progress.

This is not uncommon for teams, they will experience pressure, disruptions, or additional responsibilities. Effective leaders are aware of these pressures and understand the importance of maintaining the continual rhythm of the team in order to maintain its focus on the key goals and objectives. Teams with unrelenting focus and the time and resources to accomplish their goals can do very impressive things. Establishing rhythm may seem easy in theory but without the dedication of the leader it often gets overlooked due to competing pressures or priorities. Leaders who understand the need to protect this time and space for their teams can achieve great things for their teams and its members.

Reciprocal Accountability

While great teams maintain a consistent rhythm of revisiting their goals, progress, and outcomes, they also are keenly aware of the mutual edification they provide to one another. **Great teams include a climate and culture in which each member serves to bring their individual assets to the team while also gaining the benefits offered by the other individual members of the team and the team as a whole.** Much like the biblical proverb, "As iron sharpens iron, so one person sharpens another." When teams experience a strong sense of reciprocal accountability the individual members focus heavily on their contributions to the team while also holding others accountable for their contributions.

Much like a great football team where every person on the field knows their position and their role, yet also relies very heavily on his teammates to do the same, so is reciprocal accountability. Each team member organically holds each member accountable to their respective roles and responsibilities. **Great teammates approach the work of the team with a sense of deep responsibility to the team and its success.** They feel a sense of peer pressure to perform not only for themselves but also for the benefit of the team. An environment in which teams embrace reciprocal accountability is critical when ensuring a sense of engagement, and it takes thoughtful planning as to what types of personalities and competencies there are on the team.

Teams that are designed with reciprocal accountability in mind are those that take into account the aspirations and motivations of the members. Knowing that individuals are driven for team success and aspire to improve outcomes allows team members to have a common bond tying them together for mutual success.

While syncing team motivations are critical, so too is the matching of individual competencies of the team members. For example, if you have teammates that are strong in one area, but not another, it is necessary to understand that and be able to recruit their strengths in an area that best matches their competencies. Again, knowing who is on your team, their strengths and their personality types can assist in maximizing each person's competencies and talents.

Synching team talents is also very beneficial in helping to shed light on team blind spots. Each person on a team comes to the team with their specific experiences and their ways of seeing the world. When we, as leaders, are able to create an environment of care and trust, we are able to allow individuals to share their understandings with the team, giving the team insight into their ways of thinking and knowing. For the team, if we can uncover the unique realities and viewpoints of each individual team member, it allows us to expand our view of reality as a team. When we expand our views, it helps us to uncover our individual blind spots and see a bigger picture that can allow for greater success and effectiveness as a team. Teams that are able to capitalize on the strengths and experiences of each member improve the strength of the team by increasing the overall knowledge of the team.

To illustrate this point, let me share a story about recruiting and hiring the right people. When creating strong, dynamic teams, who are engaged and thrive on reciprocal accountability, it is necessary to select and include the right people. Recently, while working with a team to hire an additional member we had several candidates. Each candidate came with their respective strengths, talents, education, and experience. The candidate pool was strong. In the end, the team made the decision based on the specific experience, competencies, and the demeanor of one particular candidate. The notion behind the team's decision was that they wanted someone who was going to make them better. They wanted someone who was going to shed light on their blind spots and improve their way of thinking. They chose the candidate that was going to improve their sense of reciprocal accountability because she brought to the table skills, talents and a mindset that would help them thrive.

Developing reciprocal accountability on your team requires leaders to be thoughtful about who is on the team, their individual strengths and how they use those strengths to improve team dynamics. Strong reciprocal accountability can be a beautiful thing and, with the right people, can create strong, dynamic, and highly effective teams.

Summary

Creating great team dynamics will be the lifeblood of your organization. Recognizing the importance of motivation along with the right structures, protocols and routines will be essential in creating an engaging environment. People are motivated when they are involved in giving of themselves with a sense of personal fulfillment and purpose. As much as people need to be compensated fairly for their work, they must also be given an opportunity to contribute in ways that are meaningful and impactful. As mentioned earlier, it's not just a paycheck, it is a social exchange.

Great teams also know to set up strong structures or rules to guide their work and their behaviors. Setting up routine meetings to capture a consistent rhythm in your work will allow for continued momentum and effective workflows. Knowing who is on your team, their strengths and their capacities is also essential when working together. Using personality tests to unpack who is on the team supports a greater sense of trust and transparency when it is time to make decisions and delegate responsibilities.

As leaders it is our responsibility to establish the right social emotional climate that captures the hearts of those with whom we are working. **When we care deeply about our people and their sense of fulfillment, we are focused on understanding what motivates them and what rules of engagement, structures and protocols will allow them to bring their best selves to their work every day.**

Love in Action

- How have you thought about the social exchange between you and those you lead? What opportunities for autonomy, mastery, and purpose have you created?
  - Explore some options with your team as to how you can create opportunities for AMP.

- What have you done to get to know the personality types and capacities of those on your team? Who is on your team and how do they bring a sense of reciprocal accountability?
  - Take a leadership retreat with your team and explore your personality types and leadership styles. Ask how each of you might be able to use your strengths to compliment each other.
- How can you improve your team's rhythm and what protocols can you develop for problem-solving and decision-making?
  - Set up consistent times to meet with your teams and keep things moving forward. How often you meet and how you intentionally design your time will impact your team's productivity.
- How can you create a team with a strong sense of trust and transparency?
  - Work with your team and seek out ways that you can work together to build trust and transparency. As the leader, you have to be open. If you do not create a trustful environment, your people will never be transparent or truthful with you.

Chapter

Engagement through Well-Being

Great leaders are emotionally intelligent and they are mindful, they seek to live in full consciousness of self, others, nature, and society. Great Leaders face the uncertainty of today's world with hope: they inspire through clarity of vision, optimism, and a profound belief in their—and their people's—ability to turn dreams into reality. Great leaders face sacrifice, difficulties, and challenges, as well as opportunities, with empathy, and compassion for the people they lead and those they serve.

—*Richard Boyatzis and Annie McKee:* Resonant Leadership[40]

One of the most powerful and beautiful aspects of leadership is that it gives us an opportunity to improve the lives of others and make lives more meaningful. Leaders who understand the work of the heart and

---

[40] Annie McKee and Richard E. Boyatzis, *Resonant Leadership: Renewing Yourself and Connecting with Others through Mindfulness, Hope, and Compassion* (Boston: Harvard Business Press, 2005).

seek to lead with love can make a beautiful and profound impact on the lives of those they lead. When leaders are mindful and care for themselves, and those they have the privilege to lead, they are living their full purpose as people. At the core of our humanness is our heart and our drive to serve and to love those who are in our lives. As we step further into creating an environment in which people are engaged and give of themselves, we must know and understand how to create a healthy organization that supports the well-being of the people we lead and the organization as whole. To leading with love is the intentional action of designing the space and time for people to live and work in a state of well-being.

We see companies, schools, churches, and organizations of all sorts now recognizing the importance of supporting employee well-being. Why? Because research shows that doing so leads to greater engagement, motivation, and loyalty. Simply put, when we show our genuine care and concern for others, they return the effort. One major telecommunications company, for example, showed that they valued their employees by setting up a health and wellness center along with a birth through kindergarten childcare facility. This organization recognized that while people were working at the offices, having a place to exercise and workout either at lunch or before or after work supported their physical well-being and health. As a leader in the industry, they recognized that the demands of their work and provided people with a health and wellness center allowing people to manage their stress through working out, lifting weights, taking exercise classes, and utilizing spa services.

Beyond the health and wellness center, this organization designed and developed a state-of-the-art childcare facility to meet the needs of its working families. Parents who would have ordinarily had to pay and take their children to a day care facility were now able to stay close to their children during the day while their children received top notch childcare services.

Companies do not have to offer such services to their employees but those who can and do demonstrate their commitment to the well-being of their people. Supporting health and wellness and caring for the children of their employees is an intentional act of love. It demonstrated that the leadership of this organization is mindful and willing to make sacrifices for the betterment of others. This organization showed that love is action; it is compassion, empathy, and serving others. And while this is just one example of love in leadership, organizations big and small can do many things to support the well-being of their people.

Well-Being

Creating highly engaging environments is part of our call as leaders, and when those environments are infused with the elements of happiness and well-being we are doing what is right to serve our people. With that said, it is imperative that leaders take the time to frame a mindset of well-being, putting the foundations of happiness and contentment at work within the organization. Further, leaders must celebrate accomplishments and focus on supporting meaningful relationships within their organizations. They need to include moments of fun and play and leave time for pet projects and innovation. Also, leaders need to make time for gratitude and the things that make our work and our lives meaningful and valuable. And let's not forget that work should be challenging, and those challenges should serve to help us grow and thrive.

Create a Mindset of Well-Being

Each of us holds our own individual mindset. A mindset is sort of the operating system of our brains that has been developed through our understanding of the world and the mental habits we have developed over time. In other terms, it is the way we frame our view of the world and the underlying mental scripts that run in the background of our minds. A simple example of mindset is the way someone may look at food and the relationship they have with food. Some find food to be an art and enjoy the beautiful flavors and the delicate preparation processes. Others may view food as sustenance and a way to manage the health and well-being of their bodies. Food may be food, but the mindset of people and their relationships to food may be very different. Similar to exercise or religion or any number of topics, people have mindsets—a way of thinking and behaving according to their mental maps, beliefs, habits, and understandings.

Carol Dweck, author of *Mindset: The New Psychology of Success*,[41] makes mention of what she terms the growth mindset: The growth mindset is based on the belief that your basic qualities are things you cultivate through your efforts. Although people may differ in every which way—in their natural talents and aptitudes, interests, or temperaments—everyone can change and grow through application and experience.

When we understand mindset and the notion of cultivating the mind, as leaders, we are positioned to impact our organizations, families, and teams toward a mindset of well-being. As leaders, we can champion the mental framework of well-being in the lives of our people, which in turn creates healthier, more driven, and capable people. When we are intentional about caring for the health and well-being of our people, and we overtly promote their well-being, they serve to be more engaged in their work in knowing that they work with and for an organization that cares for them. How do we make well-being intentional? We must live it, promote it, share it, and model it.

Celebrate Accomplishments

When teams work hard together and accomplish great things, they need to be celebrated. Developing great teams takes intentional effort with a laser-like focus on team dynamics and team successes. When teams are able to adhere to a strong sense of rhythm and accountability, while employing structures and protocols that keep them focused on their goals, their efforts should be rewarded and highlighted. Celebrating teams and their accomplishments is a way in which we support their well-being and sense of meaning. Much like in our own personal lives, celebrating and recognizing our accomplishments leads to a greater sense of happiness, and so is true in the world of teaming. Recognition of team successes allows teams to capture their sense of accomplishment and embrace the meaningfulness of their work.

Celebration and recognition can come in many forms and fashions, but I would just share a note of caution here that when we celebrate

---

[41]Carol S. Dweck, *Mindset: The New Psychology of Success* (New York: Random House, 2008).

our successes they are not for the purpose of upstaging or creating competition. And while competition has its place as a motivator, true celebration comes at no cost to any other group or team. It is simply and truly a highlighting of the success of the team. Celebrating success needs to be from the heart, for the heart, and truly genuine.

Celebrating team success can be quietly internal and done in both large and small ways. Recognizing team accomplishments at weekly meetings or highlighting them at quarterly retreats are all viable. Also, small token dinners or lunches or simple getaways out of the office after work hours are sometimes necessary and genuinely human ways to acknowledge our success and enjoy the hard work together. Some of the best teams I have been a part of have embraced the notion that we work really hard together and also take time to celebrate hard together as well. Obviously, taking into consideration your climate, culture, and business are important, but in organizations all across the spectrum, from churches to manufacturing, taking time to celebrate and acknowledge our hard work together is important in creating teams that are engaged and find fulfilment in their work. As leaders, take the time to celebrate your team's success and help to support and care for your team's accomplishments.

Time for Play

Intentionally creating great team dynamics also means being thoughtful about times of fun and play. Some of the best ways to solidify relationships and bind teams together includes making room for play. As mentioned in chapter 4, play allows people to relinquish their normal roles and engage in fun together, which serves to create social connections and togetherness. Play can come in many forms and should be tailored to meet the individual needs of the team.

Teams make choices to play in all sorts of manners. Some teams do games or parties, others do trips and vacations. Recently a colleague of mine shared that she and her family went on a trip to Costa Rica sponsored by her company. Trips like this, while they may not be available to every organization, serve to help solidify relationships and create more meaningful connections. Many organizations may use company parties or even rounds of golf. Other organizations may choose spa days or other sorts of fun activities that would be relevant to those on the team. Several years ago, when starting a small team, I brought some new team members together. Knowing the individuals on the team and knowing their interests, we began with a simple round of golf. We spent the day enjoying some time together around an activity in which we all had interest. This simple act of play allowed us to get to know one another more deeply, understand each other as people, and it helped to solidify our work together in the office. Quickly our ability to play together translated into a propensity to work hard for one another and challenge one another to bring our best selves to the table. Our ability to play together sealed our relationship, making it safe to hold one another accountable and also lean on one another to make each of us better. Play is important and as the saying goes, "Those who play together stay together," because play serves to bring us together and solidify our engagement and care for one another—not to mention it's just fun!

Innovation and Pet Projects

Another way we can create stronger more engaged employees is to offer creative and innovative outlets. While recognizing that this would need to be uniquely tailored to each individual organization and it may be a challenge depending on the nature of the business in which you operate, allowing for the time and space for people to step out of their traditional roles and into an arena that offers an opportunity for innovation and pet projects can serve to invigorate individual passions and motivations. Because people are inherently driven by a sense of autonomy these types of opportunities can serve to strike passion into each individual that then carries back into their regular roles. Caution here: Be careful that these opportunities for innovation are well managed and don't serve to take away from the primary goals and objectives.

There are countless ways to accomplish carving out time and space for innovation among your people. Doing so will require you to look at your organization and its operations and be intentional about creating these opportunities for your people. One way to do that is to seek input from those you are leading. Ask. Ask your people how they can infuse innovative ideas into their roles and what types of projects, problems, or solutions they may want to work on.

A team of teachers who I led found they were having difficulty getting parents involved in activities related to their specific instructional program. The team noticed that parents were not engaged within the school community and generally disinterested in coming to the schools for any activities. This team of teachers, however, made it their pet project to create some very innovative plans for luring this specific group of parents into the schools for the purpose of creating more meaningful relationships and connections. The team recognized the specific dynamics of this community of parents and developed a cultural experience that tied into their language, heritage, and backgrounds. The team of teachers formed a committee and sought out local partnerships with members of this specific community and created a beautiful cultural celebration. The teachers brought in dancers and actors specific to the culture of the parents within the program. They connected with local restaurants for food and connected with local families to sponsor fun and games for the students and families. The event turned out to be a hit and has lasted many years after its origination.

This group of teachers were not required to host this cultural celebration. They did so because they recognized a problem and were given the autonomy to innovate a solution. This was outside their traditional roles but gave them an opportunity to create something new, exciting, and engaging. And while the project was both hard work and fun, it served to solidify the relationships between the teachers, the community, and the organization as a whole. This is just one simple example of an innovative opportunity that took place in a school setting. As leaders, if we want to give our people opportunities for meaningful and innovative work, we have to work closely with them to identify those specific opportunities and support the time and space for their innovation.

Companies like Southwest Airlines and Google are often recognized as companies that support their employees in their drive to be creative. Southwest, as mentioned earlier, allows its flight attendants to riff highly creative and humorous safety announcements. Customers often express their loyalty to Southwest Airlines because of this simple act of fun and innovation. Google has set aside time for its employees to be innovative as well. Google has a "20 percent time" philosophy that allows its employees to create and innovate solutions to problems. This time is specifically set aside to give people the opportunity to create and perfect side projects. While these examples are from corporate titans, the principles can be applied to almost any organization or group. If we care deeply about the engagement of our people, we need to spark motivation by setting aside the time and space for creative endeavors.

Promote Gratitude and Positivity

While I recognize that the notion of gratitude and positivity have become somewhat cliche at this point in our history, I am also very aware that what we know to do, is not often what we do. Much like sleep, a proper diet and exercise; people know they are essential to a healthy life, yet statistics will show us they are all too often ignored. As we have discussed here already, common knowledge does not always translate to common actions, and as leaders it is our job to set the table and be highly intentional about making gratitude and positivity a part of our everyday organizational culture. I can't stress this enough: Great organization culture starts with the leader. It starts with *you*! Leaders can display and project their gratitude and positivity in many ways, namely through communications, organizational norms, habits, routines, high visibility, personal connections, and training leaders to lead.

Being positive and sharing the things you are grateful for starts with the way we communicate with our employees, and all those for whom we are responsible. If you are writing weekly, monthly, or quarterly communications to your people, there should be mention of your gratitude for them, their contributions, and the impact they are making. Gratitude should serve to strengthen your relationship, confirm the value of people's efforts, and highlight the purpose and meaning of the work. Maybe you prefer to communicate via live meeting or send video memos. Either way, your communications to the people you are privileged to lead should include your gratitude and appreciation for their efforts and the organization's purpose.

Not only should your optimism be built into your global communications but they should be embedded and modeled in your meeting norms and organizational behaviors. As you lead teams, leave time and space for both yourself and your people to share their gratitude and enthusiasm. This simple act can serve to solidify teams and draw people more deeply together.

Several years ago, I was bringing job-like teams together from four different organizations to work together on a shared project. This had been attempted before, but the relational connections were never quite solidified, and the efforts never proved successful. This time, however, I suggested we start by sharing our gratitudes about our work and its impact. At first, my leadership counterparts politely rolled their eyes at the idea and thought it should be replaced with the typical, uncomfortable, disingenuous team building activity that research shows to be ineffective. To convince my counterparts, however, I shared the impact that sharing gratitudes had on other teams I had led, and so they half-heartedly agreed. As the teams came together, we began by sharing our genuine gratitudes for our work and the impact it had on those we served. This simple moment of gratitude, truth and optimism proved to be the start of a much more closely connected group who went on to work effectively together for several years. By starting our work together on a foundation of optimism, gratitude, and meaningfulness, we were able to till the soil for a more genuine connection. Being intentional about our gratitudes and sharing our hearts allowed us to see that we had a shared meaning and purpose to our work. And while this did not ensure perfect collaboration, it was a strong starting point that allowed us to work closely together with a more authentic and humble connection.

Building gratitude and positivity into your organizational culture is not something that can be done once at an initial meeting and then set aside. Being grateful and sharing life's optimism must become habit and routine in order to engage more deeply those you lead. There are many ways organizations, committees, departments, and the like make gratitude and optimism a regular occurrence. Some simple examples may include:

- Starting regular meetings with positive affirmations, celebrations, and/or good news is a simple way to build routine.

- Having a celebration board in a shared space where people can post positive ideas, thoughts, gratitudes, celebrations, and thank-yous makes positivity and gratitude visible.

- Developing a team project that supports random acts of kindness or paying it forward where people are giving to others or supporting a cause can build collective purpose and positivity.

- Supporting the use of thank-you cards on which people are able to write to others and share their gratitude and affirmation can add a personal touch to positivity and thankfulness.

- Food: Simply making the act of sharing food or breaking bread together a routine can serve to make people smile and add to a fun and positive culture.

While this is not meant to be an exhaustive list, finding ways to express gratitude and share positivity should be unique to you, your people, and your organizational purpose. But let there be no doubt: people are more willing to engage and give of themselves when the organizational culture supports a life of gratitude, appreciation, and positivity.

Setting routines and developing habits is imperative to supporting positivity in your organizational culture but it is also important that leaders support a positive culture by being highly visible and positive in their interactions. A leader's everyday habits and routines are observed by those she leads, and she must be a living example of what it means to be a positive and grateful person.

In order to be that example, visibility is imperative. Being seen either in person or through various modes of communication allows people to simply connect with the leader of the organization. The notion that "management" is some far-off faceless entity has to be dismantled if you want to promote engagement among your participants. Simple visibility allows that to occur. If your organization is too large to do that regularly, then make the effort to broadcast regular communications to your people. In those communications, it is certainly encouraged to recognize the mission of the work, the meaning it brings, but also be sure to elude positivity, celebrate and recognize the great work that is being done. Franklin D. Roosevelt, in the 1940s, used a simple "fireside chat" to regularly communicate and lead his country. As leaders in the twenty-first century, we can make those same efforts to connect, share optimism and let our people know they are valued.

Beyond regular communication, it is necessary to promote a positive organizational culture through measured and metered interactions with those you lead. Being in a state of self-control allows you to intentionally lead from a place of positivity. Leaders face many challenges and are responsible for solving many stressful problems, but when they lead people from a place of gratitude and optimism it is essential that they have the social-emotional intelligence to be able to manage and regulate emotions to be able to share their positivity even in the eye of the storm. Let there be no mistake here: leading with gratitude and positivity does not mean denying challenges or burying your head in the sand. It means remaining positive, learning from your challenges, and failing upward with your people.

Failing Upward

About ten years ago, a close colleague of mine, who I truly respect and admire, had taken a new role as the leader of a large organization. To this day, I lean on her for guidance and mentorship and I share this story as an example of how to grow and fail upward. She was working on a project that required the coordination of dozens of people, multiple departments, and about three thousand customers. The project spanned three days and included a high level of face-to-face contact with her customers.

Let me just say, day one was a disaster. For my colleague, it was the first time overseeing this project. When coming into her role, she relied on those who were responsible for the project in the past to know and understand how to run this event. Not knowing and understanding was her error, and she took quick responsibility for the day-one failure.

After day one, she and I met, and we diagnosed the issues that made day one such a disaster. The first problem we quickly identified was the point of entry. The "greeters," the first point of contact for customers, did not have access to real time customer and event information, therefore, customers were left uninformed and ill prepared for the event. The greeters did not have the big picture information about the event and could not accurately direct people. This created very long lines and a very ugly customer experience. The second major mistake was simple: there were not enough well-informed people as the first point of contact.

After day one, she met with all her department leaders to understand the errors and plan improvements for day two. The plan was changed dramatically. On day two she directed customers through alphabetical lines. Instead of two greeters like on day one, she now positioned five greeters who had access to real-time information about each customer and the status of their accounts, therefore, allowing us to direct them appropriately.

Day two went swimmingly! Things were far better. Her whole team felt like the event was back on track and customer service was much improved. I describe this event because my colleague had a choice to make as to how she would choose to handle this situation as a new leader. She chose to fail upward. Many leaders may have looked to blame, point fingers, or even express their disappointment. She, however, expressed that **it was OK to make mistakes but imperative that her team learn from them.**

She used this event as an opportunity to solidify her new organization by setting up a process of diagnosing and solving problems. Confidently and graciously, she walked her team through the errors that had been made and developed solutions accordingly. She implemented a new plan and made improvements collaboratively. She demonstrated the process of problem-solving in a way that respected others, captured their input, and allowed the team to grow together. This event led her team to respect her drive toward success, while also respecting her dissatisfaction with poor performance. She accepted the mistakes, but everyone was expected to fail upward so as not to make the same mistakes again.

Let us remember, when seeking to improve the engagement and well-being of those we lead we must be mindful to frame our challenges as growth opportunities. Every industry faces change and challenges. There will be errors and mistakes. Seeking solutions and correcting mistakes in a way that allows people to grow, while being accountable for their growth, furthers employee engagement and improves organizational outcomes. With that said, as a sidenote, if the same mistakes keep happening, then it may be time to examine your process and/or your people. **Again, it should be OK to make mistakes, but not OK to continue them.**

It's All about Relationships

Early in my career, one of my mentors shared this simple statement with me: "It's all about relationships." Strong, sound, meaningful relationships are an integral part of developing an organizational culture in which people are engaged and find meaningful work and personal connection. In chapter 4, I discussed some of the principles related to building strong relational connections. To briefly summarize, meaningful human connection relies on the understanding that relationships come in various forms and require intentional boundaries. Strong relationships also need time and space to grow. They need to be fostered with care, play, attention, and intentionality. Strong relationships also require effort and mutual investment on the part of each willing participant.

If we intend to build an organizational culture in which people are fully engaged and participate, we must be intentional about the relational connections we foster and grow. Our organizational habits and routines must be directed at building strong human connections and our words and actions must serve as a model.

When strong relationships are present and personal trust permeates an organization, it creates an environment of efficiency and effectiveness. In Sean Covey's book, *The Speed of Trust*,[42] he shares many examples of the organizational effectiveness that a strong relational culture creates. An organizational culture that supports

---

[42]Stephen R. Covey and Rebecca R. Merrill, *The Speed of Trust: The One Thing That Changes Everything* (New York: Simon and Schuster, 2006).

relational connectedness will operate with fluidity and efficiency because people will value and respect one another. Interactions among people will be uncomplicated and straightforward and obstacles will be easier to overcome. Building strong relational connectedness within an organization simply *greases the wheels*, so to speak. It makes all things easier, seamless, less complicated, and efficient. Building a culture of relational connectedness will serve well to engage people in meaningful work and mutual edification.

Pass On to Your Leaders

Creating a culture of engagement and well-being in our organizations requires an intentional focus on the elements of relationship building, gratitude, positivity, growth, creativity, and fun. These cultural elements don't happen by accident, however, and they must be modeled and expected among those you are charging to manage your organization. While hiring the right people to lead your organization is imperative—and will be discussed further in chapter 9—modeling for and training your managers will ensure that a focus on well-being will permeate all levels of the organization.

Ensuring that your managers are focused on employee motivation requires each of us to model this practice with our own management teams. We need to celebrate our accomplishments as a leadership team and ensure our mindsets include positivity and gratitude. We need to make time for play to allow for more cohesive working relationships. Our managers should also be given the opportunity for innovation and creativity within their own realms of responsibility. While modeling these organizational habits and behaviors, you should express that these are the expectations as to how your managers should lead. What you model for your leadership team should serve as an example for your managers as to how they should treat those with whom they are entrusted. Again, leadership matters, and what we model becomes part of the organizational culture. If we model the elements of well-being and care for our people, we will in turn receive the benefits of their well-being.

While modeling organizational well-being is part of the equation in developing an engaged workforce, clear expectations and oversight are also key elements in ensuring that intentional well-being is a priority. Designing a framework for your leadership team that outlines the key elements of well-being will allow your managers to be well educated and aware of the expectations. Again, ensuring you have people on your leadership team who value employee well-being and engagement will be critical to your efforts. It is also necessary to train and educate your leaders in the matters of well-being in order to maintain the focus.

Summary

Just as caring for ourselves is important to a vibrant and meaningful life, so too is tending to the well-being of our organizational culture. If we desire to have a workforce that is engaged in the mission of the organization, we must be intentional about the well-being of the people who give of themselves for the mission.

Developing a mindset of well-being that is routinely reinforced through celebrations, play and relationship building will serve to create engaged employees. Investing in our human capital in a way that supports their growth and autonomy by providing opportunities to fail upward and delve into innovative projects will capture the basic elements of human motivation and drive.

Finally, getting the right people on your management team and sharing the elements of well-being throughout your organization will serve to promote a vigorous and positive culture that permeates the entire operation.

Love in Action

- Is there a mindset of well-being in your organization? Would those who work in your organization characterize your organizational culture as positive? How can you offer opportunities for innovative projects that promote creativity and autonomy?
    - Put together an action plan that holds you and your team accountable to including positivity, celebrations, gratitude, innovative projects, and play into your organizational culture.

- How would your employees describe failure? Is failure punitive or is there room for growth opportunities and iteration?
  - Survey your people and/or gather focus group data on this topic. Remember: it is our work as leaders to create an environment that allows people to make mistakes, but they must be accountable for learning through those mistakes.
- Does your leadership or management team have the same drive for employee engagement as you? Do they need a framework for well-being?
  - Collaborate with your leadership team and develop a framework that describes your goals, outcomes, and action steps for developing an organizational culture that supports the well-being of the people who serve the organization.

Chapter

Mentorship—Building Team Strength

If you want to change the world, invest in helping another person to reach his or her potential.

—*John Maxwell*

I have often struggled with the notion that we are "self-made"—that is, that our individual and singular efforts are solely responsible for our success. And while I can certainly appreciate the virtues of hard work in creating our personal successes, I would also submit that throughout our lives each of us have had many who have invested in us. Whether those people were teachers, parents, coaches, pastors, aunts, uncles, grandparents, or mentors; each of us has had someone invest in our lives. These people often provide organic investments in language, knowledge, values, virtues, mindsets, and expectations. Over time these investments, along with our own motives, serve to form the individuals we chose to become. There is a symbiotic relationship between those who invest in us and our own self-determination that leads us through our personal journeys.

In seeking to engage those we lead, we must choose to make investments in their lives in order to create the genuine human connections that bind us together for a common goal. Much like reciprocal accountability, when we invest in the lives of those on our teams we make the entire team stronger. The Chicago Bulls won six championships in the 1990s. They were led by coach Phil Jackson, Scottie Pippen, and the infamous Michael Jordan. While Michael Jordan has certainly been recognized as the superstar of the team, many know he could not have won six championship rings on his own. He was only able to do so because he invested in those around him. His highly competitive nature led him to constantly challenge and motivate his teammates to become better. Both Coach Jackson and Scottie Pippen would attest that Jordan dug deep into the work of creating a championship team and served to mentor and coach his fellow teammates. As the trio continued through the nineties, the team was not only known for Jordan's outstanding skill but the way the team played together. They had worked together to develop an offensive scheme that included everyone on the court and that held each person accountable to their roles. The Bull's six championships in eight years did not happen by accident. It was a testimony to teamwork, engagement, coaching, and mentorship. One of the most successful franchises in NBA history recognized these important elements, and in our work it would serve us well to do the same.

Why Mentorship?

As mentioned in chapter 2, mentorship is a form of service and giving to others. It is a way in which we can invest in those around us to improve their lives and our organizations. I have been blessed to have had many great mentors in my career who have become part of my life and my leadership journey. Being grateful for those mentors has also led me to wanting to give to others so as to share the things that I have been given. In this chapter, I would like to share the key elements of mentorship, which will allow us to impact the lives of those we lead.

In the late 2000s, I had three great mentors who would inevitably change the way I approached my work, my values, and my vision for running a great organization. Two of the three were formal mentors who took the time to invest in me and share their leadership journeys. They were seasoned veterans in their professions and had experienced years of success within their organizations and on the larger stage. What is most notable about each of these wonderful mentors was the way in which they set aside intentional time to support and assist in my professional growth and success. The components of their mentorship were succinct, and they offered tremendous insights.

Both of them set aside specific and designated time for their mentorship. Our monthly meetings created a consistent rhythm of accountability and they focused on key frameworks, concepts, and philosophies of our work. Further, they both shared the keys systems, structures and protocols that led their organizations to run smoothly and efficiently. Beyond these elements, each of them also shared their vision of success where they could both identify tangible manifestations of their vision. They were able to articulate their visions and share how their visions had come to life.

I recall on one such occasion where one of my mentors spoke about her vision of creating a closely connected staff. She shared how she conducted staff meetings where seats were intentionally arranged to connect people and bring people together who may not know one another. She also mentioned that, in seeking a relational culture, she would direct people from various departments to share information about their projects in order to connect names and faces to the work. While this is a quick example, it is a clear example of a vision of success supported by the intentional implementation of systems and protocols to achieve that vision. Her sharing this example allowed me, as the mentee, to think differently about my own team and how I may want to improve their relational connectedness.

The two formal mentors I had were certainly a blessing and provided me with immense learning. Additionally, I had a third mentor who was more informal who was able to provide me with some very valuable on the job training in very specific leadership situations. Much like my two formal mentors, he was a seasoned veteran. His experience, wisdom and prudence were invaluable. And, because I was able to work alongside him daily I was able to capture the learning within many, what we called, *teachable moments*. We were able to discuss our problem-solving strategies in a less formal and more spontaneous manner. Many of our conversations dealt with real-time situations that were occurring in our organization, and because he had such vast experience he was able to provide perspective I did not have at that time. The situations and conversations we shared were extremely valuable, and this form of informal mentorship provided great life lessons that led to my future successes.

I share these brief examples because, as leaders, mentorship matters. It is how we give back to those on our teams. **Mentorship builds team strength. It exemplifies our caring for each individual's success while striving for success as a team. Mentorship serves to create an engaging culture in which people are excited to work and grow. People who experience effective mentorship recognize that the leaders within the organization care about them and their successes. Mentorship serves to be a valuable social exchange; it is an investment in care and love, and it pays dividends. Like the Bulls of the nineties, mentorship served to build an organization in which everyone was invested in the success of the team, and each team member served to make every other member better.**

Mentorship Builds a Team

Creating effective and successful organizations requires teammates who have the right character and competencies. Each team member brings their individual skills to the group for the benefit of the group while also experiencing some reciprocal benefits. Individuals serve the team and the team, in many ways, serves the individual. Teams offer connectedness, collaboration, and opportunities for success. The individual offers their skills, competencies, perspective, and resources. In order for both the team and the individual to be effective and successful, an investment must be made to strengthen each team member.

When we invest in the members of our team it strengthens their competencies and in turn improves the performance of the team. Mentorship requires us to identify the key skills and competencies necessary to do the job then designing a learning curriculum around those skills. For example, if you are leading a marketing team and the team requires a deeper understanding of marketing analytics for improved marketing strategy, mentorship should focus on those particular understandings. Or let us say you are leading a team of teachers and you need to focus on creating an effective social-emotional climate in the classroom. The focus of your mentorship would be directed toward those key skills. Further, if you are involved in process management, you would zero in on key components of the process for improved performance. There are countless examples across all industries, but the point here is this: **As mentors, we want to focus on key skills and competencies that will improve the performance of the individual and the team.**

To continue with the Chicago Bulls analogy, Coach Phil Jackson said: "The strength of the team is each individual member. The strength of each member is the team." Again, developing strong effective teams requires investment in our players. When we invest in those players through coaching and mentorship, we strengthen our team.

Mentorship Builds Shared Leadership

While mentoring and investing in individuals serves to strengthen teams it also builds the leadership capacity within members of your team. Being on a team with a shared mission, with highly competent and passionate individuals, driven to succeed, is an invigorating experience; but building those team dynamics requires that each person play a role in leading and supporting the team. Mentoring and coaching serve to infuse leadership skills in each team member, which in turn strengthens each member's ability to grow, learn, and experience empowerment. When we invest in our team members, their competencies grow, which in turn supports their confidence and sense of accomplishment. As their confidence and competencies grow, they are able to contribute more to the team, thereby experiencing a further sense of empowerment that serves to promote a sense of accomplishment and well-being. It is the snowball effect; the notion is really quite simple and in alignment with *Leading with Love*. When we invest in others, when we treat others the way we want to be treated, and when we invest in their professional growth, they are more apt to thrive and flourish, which leads to greater team success and organizational effectiveness. The recipe is not rocket science, but as Derek Sivers shares: "If information was the answer we would all be billionaires and have six pack abs." Meaning, that information alone does not change behavior. As leaders we must be intentional about investing in our people. Action item: mentor your people!

Mentorship Builds a Succession Plan

When considering a mentorship program, it is important to recognize that when we mentor we are building the future of our organization. Like any major league sports team, we should always be in the process of talent development. Improving the human capital on our team serves to elevate the performance of the whole team.

When we examine our players, we often recognize who is playing first string and who is second and third. Our role as leaders is to carefully consider our talent, examine their place on the team and utilize our starting players to assist in mentoring our second and third string players to eventually become our starters.

As you may have experienced in your own leadership journey people often move, shift, or change roles over time. With a solid mentorship program, you can preplan for these occurrences and have in place a succession plan. When we invest in our people, it allows us to build up our pool of human capital to be able to adapt to such changes while at the same time displaying our value for our teammates. Investing in our people shows them that we care for them and their future, and it allows us to plan for the future of the organization.

The Tactics of Mentorship

Starts with Vision

When we set out to assist in the growth of others through mentorship, we start with a vision of success and the skills and competencies needed for that vision. We must know what success looks like and what it requires to achieve it. In the business of public education, teachers and principals have a set of core competencies that when achieved lead to solid instructional practice and effective teaching. When teachers are mentored, the foci are those core competencies that every teacher must have in order to be effective. Teacher mentorship is then designed around specific core competencies designed to strengthen the teacher's skills and support their effectiveness.

The necessary component here is starting with a vision of success. While teachers have a clear set of core competencies for their unique profession, it is important that in your business and/or organization that you have a vision of successful performance as well. This may require the development of a framework of skills and competencies that are necessary for effectiveness.

Developing a framework for your vision will require you and your team to think deeply about your vision of a successful teammate. This will require a very specific examination of the types of skills, competencies and characteristics needed to be successful in your organization. While each profession may have unique demands, a general framework aligning to key skills, competencies, and characteristics may be a perfect place to start.

Your team should start by identifying the technical skills required to do the job. These may be very specific skills related to the work, such as financial skills, marketing skills, communication skills, and the list could go on and on. Beyond the specific skills related to the work, you will also want to ensure that your framework includes the specific character skills related to the role. I have seen too often people who have the skills but not the character. Too many times people can answer the call from a technical perspective but cannot connect or communicate with their colleagues to get the job done.

As you build your mentoring plan think first about your vision of what a successful team member looks like. What skills do they need? What competencies do they require to be successful? Then think about the type of character you need to fit your team? What social emotional skills do they require? Do they need to be humble? Do they need to be a good listener? All these questions relate to the vision you and your team must have when developing a successful team.

Developing Key Skills and Competencies—Tools of Leadership

Each sector of our professional landscape requires different skills and competencies. Across the board from agriculture to zoology, nursing to marketing, IT to sales, the various sectors of the economy require specific expertise and abilities that support organizational effectiveness. As leaders in any arena, it is our responsibility to provide an effective mentorship program that supports our people and strengthens their abilities.

As a team you may want to start by unpacking the job description to pull out the skills that need to be honed. If you do not have a job description, you may want to start by developing one that outlines the key abilities necessary for the work. Once the key skills have been identified, you will need to create a learning plan, which outlines the specific learner outcomes that are desired and the activities that will support the learning.

Let me share a quick example to illustrate. In creating a job description for a community outreach liaison, the following necessary competencies were identified:

Community Outreach Liaison	
Key Skill • Ability to develop clear written and oral communications • Identify and direct needed resources to community members	
Learning Outcome	Mentoring Activity
• The community outreach liaison will produce clear written and oral communications.	• Mentors will model clear written and oral communications with mentee. • Mentor will provide feedback on written and oral communications to improve effectiveness.
• The community outreach liaison will create a website, which informs community members of the availability of local resources.	• Mentor will provide website development support • Mentor will support metric analysis related to website effectiveness and offer feedback on a weekly basis.

Community Outreach Liaison	
• The community outreach liaison will develop weekly communications that inform community members of upcoming events and activities.	• Mentor will review and provide feedback on a biweekly basis related to the quality and effectiveness of the weekly communications.

Designing an intentional learning plan for your mentee is critical to their success and it should include specific outcomes for the mentor and mentee to achieve. The learner outcome is designed to be a specific skill or competency that the mentee will achieve. It is the quality or competency needed to be successful in their role. The mentoring activity is the learning experience designed to support the learner outcome. The mentoring activity should be the specific actions that the mentor will conduct to serve and strengthen the mentee's ability to achieve the learner outcome. This format can be adjusted to include specific timeframes and job specific qualitative or quantitative metrics of success. Your plan should also take into consideration the unique characteristics of your industry as it relates to time, context, conditions, resources, character, and skills.

While developing the learning plan, it is necessary to prioritize specific learner outcomes. Allow less significant skills to be set aside and be sure to elevate and capture the most important skills. Oftentimes the mentee-mentor learning plan will include lesser skills that take away from the effectiveness and focus of the plan, therefore, an intentional focus on essential skills and abilities is imperative when creating an effective plan.

Supporting Character, Integrity, and Trust

The act of mentorship serves as an investment in your team and your organization; and developing a solid learning plan will serve as an essential tool in supporting your players. While developing a learning plan, it is also necessary to take into consideration the *character* of each team member, and as leaders and mentors it is our job to identify and strengthen those characteristics we expect our employees to embody. It starts by identifying the character traits that will serve the team and the organization. And while certain industries require certain personal qualities, there are some general traits that serve well on most teams, which may include: collaborative, team player, problem solver, resourcefulness, motivated, and emotional intelligence—that is, self-awareness, empathy, social skills, self-regulation. When designing a mentorship program, these are potential character traits you will want to focus on when strengthening and improving your team.

As you design a plan, it is important that you are highly transparent in your intent. Be very specific about the learning outcome, include the details about the character trait you are looking to strengthen. For example, if you are wanting to strengthen a person's sense of self-awareness or emotional intelligence you would indicate that within the learning plan. The learner outcome could read: *The "Job Title" will display a heightened level of social emotional intelligence and self-awareness*. Developing a mentoring activity within the learning plan might then include the person taking the Myers-Briggs personality test and examining the results together as mentor and mentee. This will allow the mentee an opportunity to examine their character traits and discuss their understanding of themselves and their personality.

While this is just one quick example, the point here is that a learning plan should include specific learner outcomes and mentor activities focused on desired character traits. Those mentor activities may also include professional teachable moments, direct instruction, story sharing and simulations. Each of these exercises can help support teammates in their development of character and competencies.

When developing team trust and integrity, it is absolutely necessary to capitalize on teachable moments when challenging situations arise. Let me share an example. Several years back I was working closely with a team that placed a premium on trust. The team was efficient and effective. They trusted each other both technically and relationally. Each member had strong skills to get their jobs done and they held their relational connectedness in high regard. On one specific occasion, there was a breakdown in communication that led a team member to share some half truths about a timeline of events. With these half-truths came incorrectly placed responsibility for the breakdown on another team member. As the situation unfolded, I had to both mentor and mediate the situation to bring some resolution. In doing so, I used the situation as a teachable moment to mentor the individual who had shared some half-truths. I explained to him the errors that were made and how it impacted the team. I also explained to him that by purposefully sharing incorrect information he had damaged trust. Not only had he damaged his trustworthiness from a competency standpoint but then he had also damaged his reputation from an integrity standpoint. Unpacking this situation was important to do with this mentee and it led to some experiential growth. He recognized his error and experienced the implications. He learned that by owning up to his errors and taking full responsibility for them he is able to maintain his integrity while learning from the technical error.

Mentoring for character growth is important and will pay dividends in the long run in developing a team's strength of character. Developing a sound learning plan designed for strengthening specific character traits is required while also taking advantage of teachable moments. Additionally, the use of storytelling, direct teaching and simulations will all serve as teaching methods that can strengthen desired character traits. Mentoring for character growth is essential and requires intentionality, but in the end it will strengthen your team, engage your people, and the investment in others will pay off.

Develop a Rhythm of Consistency—Regular Time and Place

Several years back I wrote an update to my staff about the importance of developing a consistent time and space for improving their craft. I used this analogy: Imagine you are going on a weeklong vacation and in order to save some space in your suitcase you decide to limit some of your toiletries. In your wisdom, you decide to leave behind your toothbrush and toothpaste. In your rationale, you calculate that if, on average, you brush your teeth twice a day for approximately two minutes each time, that is in total four minutes a day of teeth brushing. Extrapolate that over seven days and you have a total of twenty-eight minutes of teeth brushing to keep those pearly whites in good shape. So you go ahead and decide if you just brush your teeth for twenty-minutes minutes prior to your departure for that weeklong vacation you can save the space in your luggage (I know it's a goofy analogy, but it makes the point). And while from a purely mathematical standpoint this may equate, we know (at least, I hope we know) that this would not be the best possible approach to our oral hygiene.

Oral hygiene is not best practiced as a single act of intensity that takes place once a week. It is best practiced as small intermittent acts of consistency that take place over long periods of time that add up to a solid oral health care plan. Mentorship is quite the same idea. Mentorship does not occur in one large act and then is set aside. Quality mentorship and the development of our human capital takes place over long periods of time while meeting and digging into learning experiences on a regular basis.

Developing a strong learning plan that supports the mentee requires regular meetings either weekly, biweekly, or monthly. The mentor-mentee relationship requires the same rhythm of accountability described in chapter 6.

Consistently throughout my work and personal life I have sought both formal and informal mentorship opportunities. Early in my career, I sought to grow and move forward in my leadership capabilities and the organization I was working for was gracious enough to allow me to support a formal mentorship opportunity with a long standing experienced and successful principal. I partnered with my mentor, Kelly, for an entire year and our time together allowed for both structured mentorship and loosely organized mentorship. Even with that sort of approach, one thing that never changed was the regularity in which we met. Our meetings were monthly, and each meeting was aligned to the learning plan. Elements of the plan, generally speaking, were focused on systems management, developing human capital, program design, and leadership. But the effectiveness of the mentorship program hinged on the fact that Kelly and I got together regularly to maintain our relationship and our rhythm.

With our regular time and space also came a sense of reciprocal accountability. Parenthetically, we were a good match and our personalities meshed well together. This allowed for the trust and understanding that supported the natural elements of reciprocal accountability. As a mentor, she could see I valued this experience and came ready to learn. This propelled her to want to support me and provide me with a rich learning experience. Knowing that Kelly was going to bring her a game, I had to come prepared. I knew our time was important, and I came to each of our meetings with my proverbial homework done and ready to go. Throughout that very meaningful year, we developed a nice friendship, strong trust, and I believe we both benefited from this formal mentoring program. It strengthened Kelly's intentional understanding of her own work and it strengthened my professional capacities. This didn't happen by accident. It happened because two people were intentional and dedicated to regular, consistent, and meaningful mentorship that focused on professional growth and improvement. There was a solid, collaboratively designed learning plan, and each person brought their attention and drive for professional and personal advancement.

Tough Love

Knowing that mentorship is designed to grow and build the people within your organization does not exclude us from some tough and challenging experiences. Love is not always easy. It certainly comes with its hard conversations and unpleasant experiences, but positioning tough love for growth and progress is a critical perspective that we must maintain. Take, for example, the raising of a child. If you are a parent, you can certainly empathize. When raising our children, there is immense love and care. We want desperately for what, we believe, is best for them. Sometimes this may include having some tough and uncomfortable conversations with our children about such ideas as persistence or perseverance in the face of adversity. I remember my daughter's first few weeks of college. She was entering a new life at a new university and was nervous, had some doubts and was missing her friends. As she shared those trepidations with me, I had to press back on her a little and explain that things are not going to always going be easy. Change can be difficult and situations that lead to our growth and progress take effort and hard work. The alternative to working hard is living a life of defeat, weakness, meaninglessness, and default. I can't say she listened intently with wonder and amazement at my infinite wisdom. She did not! Rather she may have preferred to be coddled and nurtured in a way that only justified her fears, but I was unwilling to let her quit without considering the repercussions. I had to have some tough love conversations with her over those first few weeks of school. I had to keep her focused on the long-term growth and possibilities that a college degree would provide and steer her away from her short-term fears and apprehensions.

Much like parenting, leaders who lead with love must know that there are tough conversations to be had. Those conversations, while difficult, are designed for growth and transformation. Imagine I had done nothing with my daughter, and she felt justified to quit school and come home defeated by her challenge. Would that have been an act of beneficial love? That would have been giving into her fears and not challenging her to grow. Our work as leaders is to challenge people to grow! Not only for themselves but for the benefit of the organization as well.

Tough conversation, with our children, as well as our mentees, are required and are part of the overall improvement process. When we approach tough love conversations, however, we must keep in mind a few simple ideas: 1) Tough love is more about love than tough. 2) Tough love should be tough on concepts or principles. 3) If you have to use anger or emotional leverage to be tough, you're probably not clear in your principles, so you may want to redesign your plan. 4) All lessons should be captured in a learning plan for intentionality.

To start, when we talk about tough love it is important to understand that tough love is not about the mentor being hard on the mentee in the sense that this is not the typical football coach yelling at the player to toughen up. Mentorship, again, is about the care and investment in another person for mutual edification. When we view mentorship with a mindset of compassion and personal growth, we are positioned to support and build up our mentee. The tough portion comes into play when we are pushing our mentees to expand their skills, knowledge, capacities, and personal characteristics. It is important that we challenge our mentees and make the learning process valuable. It should be a challenging and tough experience.

If we want to make the learning process valuable and rich we must understand that love comes first. It must be understood within the relationship, and intentionally stated, that the mentee-mentor relationship is a safe place that is designed for experiential growth and progress. The purpose of the mentor-mentee relationship should be described as supportive, intentionally challenging, and purposed for growth. The experience should be designed to stretch individual capacities, but the love and support comes first.

While the mentor-mentee relationship and purpose are steeped in care and compassion, let there be no mistake: the experience should be composed of challenging experiences designed to strengthen capacities, knowledge, and character. Second, the mentor-mentee relationship experience should be relentless in learning the necessary principles and essential concepts. The learning plan should include experiences that serve to build the mentee and strengthen their competencies in a way that aligns to the purposes of the organization. If, for example, you're learning plan is focused on strengthening employee ethics, the learning plan should include specific outcomes that require the mentee to demonstrate honesty, integrity, and the ability to serve the customers ethically. In designing your mentorship programs, being specific about the tough and challenging lessons you require should be well articulated and succinct with the desired outcomes of the plan. As mentioned previously, the plan should include explicit understandings and outcomes that allow the mentee to visualize the outcomes and be able to prepare for the road ahead. To say in another way, tough love is about being tough on principles and learning outcomes, and thoughtful and caring about the mentee.

Third, it is important to self-regulate and be sure you do not let your own emotions serve to drive the mentorship experience. I share this based on experiences I have had and witnessed as mentors and/or leaders who are poorly principled and who led with emotional charge. Leading in such a way is dangerous and is often an indicator of poor leadership, lack of planning and a lack of self-control. In contrast, the mentor-mentee experience should be well outlined and succinct, and it should be captured in a learning plan that is well thought out and organized for specific outcomes.

Let me share an example to illustrate how *not* to lead with emotional charge. Several years ago, I witnessed a leader who was mentoring a small group of principals. He had given unclear directions for a specific communication process. How do I know it was unclear? Because each of his mentees got it wrong. In the midst of the communication error, he became highly emotionally charged to the point of berating a few members of his team. It was ugly to watch, and it created long lasting damage to his respect among team members and his reputation. John Maxwell, author of *The Five Levels of Leadership*, would say that he went from a level four leader back to a level one leader all in one day. One simple act of emotional instability and unchecked emotional control led to a deep cut in the culture of his team. This situation could have been easily remedied if the expectations were clear and succinct and if the error was met with a need for understanding rather than a temper tantrum. As leaders and as mentors, it is vitality important we lead with poise, composure, and measured emotions. To that end, we must be well planned, communicate intelligibly, and be succinct in our expectations. And if we are not, own the problem and work with people to solve the issue with balance and equanimity.

In sum, as mentioned above, our mentor experiences should be intentional. Meaning, they are well planned and specific about the outcomes we desire for our mentee. The expected outcomes of our mentorship program should be captured in a learning plan and prepared with specificity. **Remember: *Tough Love* is tough on the principles. It is clear in its lessons. It is succinct on the outcomes being required. Tough love is about intentionally designing challenging experiences that lead to increased growth in the competencies and capacities for those we are leading and mentoring.**

Empower Your Mentees—Adult Learning Theory

Some of the greatest gifts we can offer to others is our experience, knowledge, and understandings of our work and/or our profession. Sharing allows us to strengthen others to become the next generation of leaders. Hopefully, those leaders will be as careful and as thoughtful as we intend to be, with a heart for people and their success. **We should ensure that our mentorship program is designed to ignite motivation and empower our mentees for the work we share.** We do this through purposeful preparation and the equipping of our mentees for their road ahead. We design intentional learning plans that serve to strengthen our mentees, enabling them to succeed and contribute to the organization at large. We support the development of their skills and competencies in such a way that they become empowered and confident leading to greater motivation and drive.

Remember: what drives and motivates people is their own ability to take ownership and mastery over their own lives. Our job as mentors is to support them in this effort so they can become energized and inspired. Our intentional focus, our use of the learning plan, and our ability to capitalize on teachable moments are all purposed to encourage and elevate our mentees. We are seeking to build them up allowing them to see new insights that will lead to their success and greater contributions to the team. Mentorship, while succinctly focused on skills and competencies, must also be well intentioned for empowerment, energy, and motivation.

As we design learning experiences that lead to greater empowerment, we must also keep in mind how adults learn and take these elements into consideration as we design our plan:

- Adults need to know the *why*. Our mentees should understand why they are learning a specific concept or skills and where it fits into their overall role.

- Adult learners have a need for autonomy and self-direction. While we develop a learning plan we must also be thoughtful of allowing our mentees to direct their own learning and have choice in those matters when possible.

- Adult learners need to have learning experiences that reflect the work they perform. Learning activities should mirror the work they are expected to accomplish.

- Adult learners are in tune with what they need to know. Give them knowledge and understandings that are valuable and meaningful. Limit the "fluff."

- Adult learners need to apply. Adults often come with strong foundational knowledge and understanding; therefore we have to design experiences that lead to application of knowledge and skills. Mentors should be "doing."

- Adult learners are both intrinsic and extrinsic learners. They are motivated by knowing how this new knowledge or skill will help them succeed and master their work.

Books as Mentors

I want to add here the importance of book study when learning as a team and mentoring our teammates. Tim Ferris, in two of his books, *Tribe of Mentors*[43] and *Tools of Titans*[44], emphatically demonstrates that the reading of and reflection on leadership and the growing of our capacities is essential to improved performance and effectiveness. As mentors and as leaders, we need to utilize the vast array of resources available to us, and getting our mentees involved in book study fosters and supports their growth and success. I can empirically attest that when we dig deep into a mentor book focused on the skills and capacities we are intending to grow great things can happen. On many occasions, using books as mentors has allowed myself as a mentee, a mentor, or a team lead, to not only grow as a person myself but also watch my team grow in ways that I may have never expected.

When we use mentor books to open up conversation, it brings forth dialogue that may not have otherwise been discussed. It leads teams to new insight and new perspectives. Mentor books may bring to light specific skills, concepts, or ideas that may not have been intentioned and yet lead to individual growth.

Another beauty about mentor books is that they lead to the triangulation of conversation and mentorship. What I mean by that is, books welcome in another's ideas into the mentor-mentee relationship that will allow for less direct mentorship. The nature of the mentor-mentee relationship can, at times, be just a two-

[43]Timothy Ferriss, *Tribe of Mentors: Short Life Advice from the Best in the World* (Boston, MA: Houghton Mifflin Harcourt, 2017).
[44]Timothy Ferriss, *Tools of Titans: The Tactics, Routines, and Habits of Billionaires, Icons, and World-Class Performers* (Boston, MA: Houghton Mifflin, 2017).

way street where the mentee seeks the mentorship of the mentor. Meaning, it is just the two of you. When you invite in another author, however, you allow for a third member who can add to the conversation. This third member can open up dialogue in new ways and allow for less direct teaching and more open thinking and philosophical discussions. I have been a part of these conversations on many occasions and they can truly be eye-opening. Bringing forth a concept or idea from a book and discussing the idea with openness and inquisitiveness can lead both the mentee and mentor to open up their minds and accept new information that can change the ways they see their work and their world.

With that, I encourage the use of books as mentors. Book study can be a highly effective experience and one that supports growth in exciting and unexpected ways. (The texts that have been provided in the footnotes of this book may be a place to start if you are looking for ideas.)

Summary

When we seek to mentor, we do so with the intention of building our team and our supporting cast. Mentors must work to lay out a highly intentional learning plan that will support the skills and competencies of the mentee in a way that leads to their understanding and application of those skills and competencies. The mentorship experience should be well planned, and regular time and space should be set aside to ensure the integrity of the learning experience. Mentees should be challenged, and their experiences should be tough as well as empowering. As mentors, with a heart for others, we must lead by example and be intentional about strengthening the ethical character of our mentees. Book study can add some uniquely rich learning to the mentorship program you design and should be well considered when crafting your plan. Ultimately, let us not forget our purpose. Mentorship is for the good of others. We are seeking to build and strengthen those around us to reinforce our team and improve the quality of our work together.

Love in Action

- What skills and competencies does your team require and what is your vision of success for each individual you lead?

How would your team be different if every team member was able to contribute at their highest level while they shared in a common goal?

- o Build an organizational chart and identify where mentorship and people development would help serve to strengthen your organization.

- What will your intentional learning plans seek to instill in your mentees? What are the specific skills you want your employees to know? And how can you create learning experiences that address team character, integrity, and trust? What are the challenging and tough principles, concepts, or understandings that are essential to imparting upon your team? How will you design learning experiences that will stretch and grow your employees' skills sets?

- o Create a learning plan for your mentees. Use the example above and capture the skills, competencies, and dispositions you would like to develop.

- What structure will you design that will ensure consistency in your mentorship program? How can you ensure that mentorship is regularly scheduled on your calendar?

- o Create a mentorship calendar. Ensure that your mentor-mentee meetings include a rhythm of consistency.

- What great books can you use to assist in your mentorship program? How can you use mentor books to spark new and creative ideas and perspectives?

- o Identify a few great books—many have been included in this writing—and do a book study with your mentees and leaders. It can lead to powerful conversations and growth.

Part III

Love as a Verb

Chapter

9

Hire Quality People

There is nothing better than being on a shared mission with extraordinary people, who can be radically truthful and radically transparent with each other.

—*Ray Dalio*

In part I, we focused on the elements of *loving thyself* with the understanding that it is essential that we come to our seat of leadership with a focus on personal health and well-being. We must be centered and have a deep understanding of our purpose and our *why*. We must be intentional about our personal welfare, and we must have in place strong habits that support our personal and professional effectiveness. It is essential that we lead from a place of personal strength, with our vessels full, positioned to lead others with vigor, clarity and with a sense of purpose.

Part II focused on *loving thy neighbor* by strengthening our organizations through employee engagement and people development. By ensuring that we have a shared purpose behind our work, with a focus on building and strengthening our teams, we will lead our organizations to be more cohesive and effective. Being highly deliberate about designing and crafting our *WHY* together bonds us to a common purpose and goal. Further, we must design our organization around the pillars of well-being in order to develop stronger healthier teammates. Also, as we build our teams, it is imperative that we make the time and place for mentorship to ensure each member is strong and prepared to be a contributing partner on our team.

In part III, we will focus on love as action; love as a verb. I am often reminded about the nature of love and although there are certainly feelings and emotions associated with love, love is also associated with action and intentionality toward others. Love in this form is focused on bringing others to their highest good.

Parents know this form of love very well. While parents often share their immense feelings and emotional love toward their children. they also share their desire to assist and support their children in becoming their best selves—that is, parents will often put forth specific *actions* that will lead to the well-being of their children. On occasion, good parenting may include teaching right habits and skills or possibly selecting new friends. Parenting may also include supporting our children through change and helping them design future plans. No matter the action, as parents, we support and love our children through action, and it is those actions that help our children grow and flourish.

In our organizations, we as leaders, need to be intentional about our actions and our love and care for people as well. It is our work to specifically and intentionally design and develop organizational structures that strengthen the organization as a whole.

Part III will be targeted toward designing intentional systems, structures and protocols focused on improving your organization and driving your teams toward more effective operations. This section will focus on:

- Designing systems for hiring tens: In order to design and run an effective organization, it is absolutely imperative to choose the right people to join you in your work. Having the right teammates will ultimately impact your ability to accomplish your mission. Hiring decisions may be the most important decisions you make.

- The Three Ts: Teams on Target with Tools. Developing a healthy teamwork environment with a rhythm of accountability, the ability to collaborate and support shared decision-making and creativity while also employing intentional tools that keep the team and the organization moving forward.

- Adapting to change: Developing a framework for organizational evaluation and improvement: Organizational improvement relies heavily on right thinking, aerial perspective, and leverage. Organizations require evaluation and change strategies that allow them to adapt and remain impactful.

Hire Quality People

Many of us recognize the value that work offers and put much effort into making it meaningful and worthwhile. We appreciate what we do, and we find joy in our work. In doing so, we also understand that in order to be effective we have to partner with people who value the work and its meaning in similar ways and with similar levels of drive and passion. Finding and connecting with the right people will be critically important when leading and creating a successful team or organization. As a matter of fact, having the right players on your team will ultimately determine the success or failure of your mission.

I have had the privilege of being a part of some excellent teams and organizations and I have created and designed teams by hiring and positioning people in roles that suit their skill sets. To the contrary, I have made my own mistakes and also witnessed other organizational leaders who have made poor hiring decisions. I have experienced how those poor decisions took an unnecessary toll on the team and the organization. As leaders, it is our job to hire high performers, support their growth, and let them thrive. We must take responsibility for our hiring decisions and seek to find the best people to work alongside us and our team.

Recently, I came across a podcast in which a business leader shared that he supported a philosophy that each year 20 percent of the staff should be let go to allow the rest of the organization to witness these "high expectations." He believed employees should have a healthy fear of termination in order to spark their drive and motivation. While I listened to this ill-informed theory, I thought to myself, "Do you enjoy throwing money in the toilet, and don't you have a responsibility to your stakeholders to be financially sound?" The cost of employee turnover and training, not to mention the negative impact on culture and climate, can be crippling. To this individual, however, this was the cost of doing business, a way of motivating, and a way to ensure the best were on his team. Beyond simply throwing money away each year on turnover I would challenge any leader who has this mindset: If you need to lay off a significant number of people each year, what does that say about your ability to recognize, hire, and support good talent? If you are laying off 20 percent of your people, the problem might be you, and ultimately you are hurting your organization and stifling its effectiveness.

I have also witnessed organizational leaders who have a revolving door when it comes to personnel. Each year they are hiring for the same positions only to have to either replace them the following year due to incompetence, or the employee seeks to leave. In my experience, leaders often fail to look at themselves or their hiring practices, and in so doing, fail the team and the organization by not recruiting the right talent, with the right skills, with the right mindset. It is my hope that this chapter will shed some light on ensuring that we find the right people for our teams, allowing our teams and each individual to thrive. We need to hire tens.

Hiring Tens

Finding the right talent to fit our organization is crucial in creating the right environment of our employees and supporting organizational quality. Unlike the leaders I have mentioned above, leaders who know how to hire quality people, or what I like to refer to as tens, will ultimately be setting up the organization for success. On a scale of one to ten, ten being top talent, if we are able to recruit, hire, and train tens, we set ourselves up for organizational effectiveness and strong team cohesion.

While I use the proverbial "ten" to indicate top talent, let me also share that talent may not always be a ten when it comes through your door. It may be that you are hiring people who will need training and support. But ensuring that each person has the capability, the drive and desire to be a ten is crucial. Evaluating and positioning our human resources is an important element of leadership. Identifying your top talent and knowing who your future tens will be is vital work. Good leaders know who will grow to be their top performers and where they should be positioned on the team. **Let me reiterate: knowing your talent and where it should be positioned is paramount to effective leadership.** Next up, we will look at processes and protocols for identifying top talent.

Include Your Team: Design a Job Description

When we are seeking tens we start by identifying the specific skills sets and core competencies we are looking for to meet the needs of our specific business or organization. We should take inventory of the human resource requirements and design a job description that outlines the specific skills and competencies needed to complete the job.

Being specific about the competencies you are seeking may require input from your team. Including team members in the process of designing the appropriate job description is a worthwhile cause. Let me explain. When looking for talented people and designing a job description, you and your team may quickly be able to identify the core competencies a candidate may require. By core competencies, I am referring to the specific skills that allow them to know and understand the work. This may also include specific licensure, certifications, educational degrees, and so forth. For example, if you are hiring a new member to join your marketing team, you would obviously expect them to have a technical understanding of marketing skills, analytical concepts and other technical skills specifically related to marketing. Their technical understanding of marketing and the specific skills needed to succeed on your marketing team should be relatively easy to capture on your job description.

More complicated and dynamic, however, are defining the more adaptive or human skills you and your team may be seeking. Because we often work in teams alongside other people, you and your team should be seeking to create a cohesive environment that would include specific character dispositions, such as temperament, openness, collaborative, resourcefulness, and others. These dispositions should also be considered competencies and should be captured in your job description. I will explain more about dispositions later.

Let me share a quick example: Several years ago, I was working with one of my leadership teams on hiring a new staff member. We found a highly talented candidate who came to us with mountains of experience and a very strong skill set. At the end of the interview, after the candidate had left, I simply said to the interview team: "She was strong, but do you want to work with her?" I asked that question because while her technical skills were spot on, her ability to connect and converse with the team was observably weak. The interview clearly brought out her lack of self-awareness, her inability to listen and be thoughtful when others were speaking, and I could sense the annoyance of the team in her "know-it-all" attitude. While this candidate certainly had the skills to do the job, I could confidently say that not many on the team would enjoy doing the job with her.

Understanding the core competencies necessary for the job is vitally important, but also knowing your team and developing the job description to capture the necessary "soft skills" is critical to maintaining team cohesion. Therefore, when you work together to identify the skills and attributes you are looking for, it is imperative that you collaborate with your team to ensure that your team has specifically identified what character traits the right person will embody.

Conduct Organic Interviews

When we are seeking to hire tens, we are not only looking for specific technical skills and character attributes but we are also seeking to gauge specific capacities. This means we are seeking to understand what a potential candidate may be able to handle as a team member. Often when individuals join a team there may be a skill or experience gap that exists primarily because the new member does not have the specific background associated with your team and your organization. That is not to say they don't have requisite skills; it is simply to say they may not know the inner workings of the organization. Knowing there may be such a gap we need to uncover a candidate's capacities or their potential to provide value to your team.

Gauging a potential candidate's capacities relies heavily on a thoughtful and careful interview process that seeks to understand a candidate's background and their potential to add value and skills to the organization. In many cases interview questions would allow you to uncover what challenges the candidate has faced in the past and how they have overcome those challenges. This may include questions that require the candidate to share how they managed their accomplishments, solved problems, or demonstrate their resourcefulness, just to name a few. **And while you may craft some quality questions to uncover a candidate's capacities, I would implore you to add a heavy dose of patience and careful observation within the interview process.**

Patience in the interview and recruiting process allows us to get a better knowledge of a candidate's competencies and also their capacities for growth and change. In order to gain that understanding, we must be patient and allow the candidate to demonstrate who they are naturally. Often we will interview potential teammates in an artificial environment such as a boardroom and we will ask the candidate several questions to get an understanding of their skills and their character. While this is certainly a perfect starting point, the process must go deeper in order to get a more complete understanding of the candidate.

If your screening and interviewing process includes a typical boardroom interview, that is great, but it must also include allowing opportunities for more genuine and realistic interactions among yourself and the team. **In capturing an understanding of a candidate's technical and social emotional capacities, it is necessary to take a closer look at the candidate and allow for more organic experiences to occur.**

These organic and natural experiences can come in a myriad of forms and should be most natural to you, your team, the position, and the candidate. In other words, it must be a real-world experience that allows you to get to know the person more genuinely. This may include simple things like a lunch or breakfast meeting. Breaking bread with someone can allow for more natural interaction. Depending on the nature of the position you may want to take the team out for a sporting event. These types of events can allow for very natural interaction. If you want to test the patience of a candidate, you may invite them to play a round of golf and watch how they deal with the adversity of shanking a ball off the tee. That can always be telling! I'm kidding here, but you get the idea.

Genuine and natural social interaction allows us to demonstrate our true selves and making time for experiences such as the ones exemplified above allows us to get a better understanding of a person's disposition and their ability to fit in with your team. Walking through the candidate's past experiences in a more natural, nonthreatening manner allows you and your team to be able to identify qualities that may not be uncovered in a formalized interview.

Allowing for organic conversation can allow the candidate to relax and be his or her more genuine self, which can allow you to better see and understand their capacities for teamwork, problem-solving, temperament, self-awareness, and the like. When finding the right candidate, these are some of the capacities you might be looking to uncover:

- Team player: The candidate's ability to work with and alongside other members in a healthy and mature manner.

- Problem-solving: Can the candidate be presented with a challenge and how do they go about solving the problem? Are they resourceful?

- Cooperation: A candidate's ability to work with others to grow and solve problems together.

- Growth Mindset: Does the candidate have a static view of herself and the world, or is there the mindset that she and the team can always grow and get better?

- Optimism: What is the candidate view of the future in your work and in our world? Optimistic people prove to be more effective.

- Mastery Mindset: A candidate's drive to do well and thrive in not only their work but also in life.

- Creative Outlets: What does the candidate do to improve their individual life outside the office? Knowing this can give you insight into what drives them and motivates them.

- Values: Get at the heart of what a candidate values and it will shed light on who they will be with you and your team.

- Common sense: Can the candidate be prudent? Talking through ideas and concepts can open up a window to their thinking.

- Calendar: Understanding that how the candidate uses their time gives us a window into understanding the candidate. Seeking to understand a candidate's calendar can allow us to see what they value.

- Social and emotional well-being: Candidates who have elevated to the higher levels of Maslow's hierarchy of needs—that is, *self-actualization* will many times make far better teammates due to their own self-understanding, self-regulation, and drive for purpose.

- Character: Ultimately understanding a person and their character allows you to better make hiring decisions for you and your team.

- Swag: And just for fun, do you want a little swag? Confidence can be a very attractive and persuasive characteristic. One of my previous bosses told me I got the job because of my "swag"—that is, my hair. He was bald and very much appreciated what was then a full head of hair. It's OK to have some fun with this stuff!

Gauge Experience, Aptitude, and Education

Ray Dalio, one of the world's most successful hedge fund managers, in his book *Principles*, states: "If you choose the right people with the right values and remain in sync with them, you will play beautiful jazz together. If you choose the wrong people, you will go over the waterfall together."[45] Hiring the right people is critical, and choosing poorly can really be a major tax on your team and your organization.

When seeking to find the right people, it is also important to look for experience, aptitude, and education. That is not to say there are not exceptions to the rule but finding the right candidate starts with their experience. Experience can be the greatest predictor of future success. The candidate's past experience may have given them the skills to do the job and the proving ground to showcase their competencies and their capacities. When you are vetting a new member of your team, be sure to take time to understand their background thoroughly and carefully in order to tease out their previous experiences.

Beyond experience comes aptitude. When we speak of talent, we are referring not only to the core competencies that one has acquired but also their aptitude. Similar to capacity, aptitude tends to be more aligned with one's ability to extend or grow their skills. While there may be some semantic hairsplitting here, understanding someone's capacity, meaning how much they can manage; and their talent aptitude, that is their ability to grow, are very important when examining new prospective hires.

Additionally, education is another key component to examine when looking at prospective talent. Understanding a candidate's educational background can give you an understanding of their technical knowledge and a more holistic understanding of their personhood. A candidate's educational background can give you a window into what sort of organizations a person was involved with such as charity, service, professional organizations, etc. Understanding a candidate's educational background and experience can allow you to get a clearer picture of who they are and what they value.

Education may also be valuable in determining a person's drive and motivation. How they performed in school can give us an understanding of their drive and motivation to perform well and

---

[45]Ray Dalio, *Principles: Life and Work* (New York: Simon and Schuster, 2017).

to achieve. Understanding a candidate's motivation level and their drive to succeed is important when choosing the right candidate, and their past educational experience can give us a glimpse of those characteristics.

What I am about to say here is simply a caution: While education is part of the overall recipe for choosing the right candidate do not let it outweigh the other elements I have described here. I have too often witnessed candidates, who were chosen because of the school or university they attended, falter because they were not the right technical or personal fit for a team. I have worked with people from well-known universities who were completely outshined by people from smaller or lesser-known schools. This is not to say there aren't some great prep programs out there, because there are, and tapping into those streams is important, as I will describe later. This is just cautionary, however. Being diligent in *all* areas mentioned here is important. Designing a hiring system for gaining a comprehensive understanding of the entire candidate, including competencies, capacities, aptitudes, experience, and education, is vital in hiring tens.

Know Thy Candidate

In chapter 6, we stressed the importance of knowing the members of our teams in order to ensure team solidarity and engagement. We discussed using specific tools to gain an understanding of each team member, their perspectives, and their skill sets. Much in the same way, I recommend using those same tools, and others more specific to your organizational needs, to capture a broader picture of the candidates you may be intending to bring on board.

Using the Myers-Briggs Type Indicator (MBTI) survey can allow you to get a deeper understanding of each candidate and allow you to see if they are a good fit for you and your team (see chapter 6 for a deeper understanding). For example, you may be looking for someone who is comfortably extroverted and needs to be able to feel alive in sales and social settings. The MBTI can give your insight into their character and reveal if the candidate is more introverted or extroverted and how they may use that to their advantage. The results of the MBTI survey can set the stage for some great conversations with your candidate, and it allows them to share their own perspective of themselves. Slight caution here: Use any screener or survey such as MBTI as a single data point. Do not use it in isolation. When getting a clearer picture of a candidate, be sure to triangulate your information and use multiple data points.

You may also choose to use the Enneagram assessment, which can give you a glimpse into a candidate's leadership style and competencies. You may be looking for specific skills and dispositions in your candidate, and the Enneagram can shed some light in that area.

The MBTI and the Enneagram are certainly not the only tools to use in the hiring process. There may be more specific tools related to your line of work and the skills sets you are looking for. For example, in education, myself and my teams have used a specific tool that allows us to get an understanding of prospective teachers and administrative candidates. The tool allows us to get an understanding of a prospective educator's skill set, their perspective on teaching and their professional disposition related to areas of teamwork, skill mastery, growth mindset and others.

Again, when we are seeking to hire tens, we want to do our due diligence to recruit the best possible people to work alongside us and our team. Doing so requires us to utilize the tools most appropriate to our industry to help us uncover the skills, competencies, and dispositions of our future teammates.

Fishing the Right Streams

At this point, we have identified the general components that must be addressed in order to hire tens. There is simply no doubt that if you want to run a great team and organization you have to hire the right people to join you on your journey. As I mentioned earlier, this may be the most critical element to your organizational success and critically examining a candidate's background is essential. Now that we know what we are looking for, we have to know where to find it; and this being a nonindustry specific will require you to have to do some research on your own in order to tap into the recruiting streams that will be most beneficial to you. Here I will briefly share a few tips:

First, use industry specific recruiting platforms and search firms. Again, I am not involved in every market; however, I am well aware that each industry has its unique streams from which to fish. Recruiting networks and online platforms that are industry specific can open the doors to prospective candidates. With that, you may flood your inbox with candidates, and that is OK. Either way, do your due diligence when screening. It was Abraham Lincoln who said, "If I had eight hours to chop down a tree, I'd spend the first six of them sharpening my axe." Preparation is worth your time. Hiring well eliminates headaches down the road.

Next, partner with trade schools and universities. Depending on the level of employee you are looking for you may consider partnering with reputable secondary schools and training programs that have proven successful in your past. When bringing on entry-level people, I have found that there have been a few university programs related to my work that have proven to provide strong and reliable results. I tap into them yearly, I ensure we have representation at their job fairs and the people I have recruited from their programs continuously succeed. I know I mentioned earlier to be careful to not overestimate someone due to their education, but remember it's just one element of hiring, and if it's a good stream, continue to fish it.

Utilize your professional network. If you are in a position of leadership, and you have developed a strong network, don't be afraid to share your hiring needs with others. I have in the past used my professional network to hire many teammates and after doing my due diligence in examining their backgrounds have found much success in that stream.

Your current employees may have networks that prove valuable when recruiting as well. Tapping into the networks of those on your team can prove successful, especially if your teammates may already know the candidate or have developed a relationship with them. In my past, this has been an essential element in hiring for difficult to fill positions. A brief example here: I had for many years a position that was turning over regularly due to licensure issues, meaning the employed needed to maintain a specific license to be able to work in this profession, and opportunities elsewhere—that is, they could write their own ticket. Their work was specialized, and their skill set was so heavily in demand that these individuals could pick and choose where they wanted to work. My turnover rate was minimally 10 percent per year. To combat this turnover, I began solely hiring people who were already connected to my current people. So, when new hires came on, they weren't just joining a team. They were working with their friends, which became like a close-knit family. This strategy proved well for me, and it allowed me to create a very cohesive working environment for this team. So much so, that although people had opportunities elsewhere, maybe even more money, they chose to stay closely connected to their team. I recognize this may not always work, but this strategy proved very successful for this specific team.

Fishing the right streams is essential, and this is by no means meant to be an exhaustive look at where to cast your line; however, hiring is critical, and it will serve you well to tap into the right networks.

Why Should Tens Want to Work for You? And What about Eights and Nines?

While we have spent this chapter digging into finding the best people for your organization there are two additional points I would like to cover briefly. First: Why would tens want to work for you?

To answer this, let's look back at the spirit of leading with love. First, tens should want to work for you because they are well aware that, as a leader, you are steeped in well-being, that you are socially-emotionally healthy, that you lead with purpose, and that you care for others as referred to in chapters 1–4. Second, tens should want to work for you because they are well aware that you seek to create a working environment that fosters individual growth and collaborative teamwork. As a leader who cares deeply about those you lead, you seek to create an organizational culture that engages employees and leads them to their greater good.

Finally, tens should want to work for you because they know they are valued. When it comes to money and benefits, that means providing a pay structure that demonstrates their value and supports their ownership in the organization. How you approach that will be determined by your industry and your resources. I do believe, however, supporting people financially, slightly north of their expectations, creates a deeper sense of engagement and demonstrates our care for our employees.

The second question I want to touch on briefly here is: What about eights and nines? When I encourage you to hire tens, that is a figurative statement to hire the best possible candidates. You may not have access to the tens. Your candidate pool may only include eights and nines or even lower. Your role as a leader is to hire the best possible candidates you can and develop an intentional hiring plan for doing so. If you don't find a ten, and you find someone who will need some additional support, that is OK. As leaders, it is our job to find the best we can, coach them, mentor them, and support them in becoming tens.

Summary—a Tale of Two Hires

Hiring tens is critical when building a high performing team. Finding the right people to join you on your journey will make for beautiful jazz or conversely, if they are the wrong fit for your team, they can make for a long tumultuous ride. Finding people who have the skills and potential to add value to your team is paramount, and interviewing them more closely to determine if they will be a right fit will ultimately lead to a team that is in sync and headed in the right direction.

I'd like to share a brief story to add to this summary. Years ago, I was working for a very large educational organization that was seeking to hire for a critical leadership position that would oversee the workings of approximately two hundred people, including several teams. The person chosen for the job was handpicked by the highest levels of the organization and was essentially placed in the role with little examination of his failed past experiences and with no voice from the team who would ultimately have to work alongside him.

The failed attempt to hire a ten in this role had enormously damaging consequences. After just a few months of working with this newly appointed leader, many of the other leaders in the organization sought employment elsewhere. Top performers left the organization. Teams broke down. Turnover skyrocketed. All this organizational damage was unnecessary and very avoidable had the top executives simply adhered to a more open, transparent, and diligent hiring process.

On the contrary, let me share with you another brief story in which hiring a ten paid huge dividends: After the individual I mentioned had upended the organization, he was eventually removed to find employment that would better suit his skills set. The next time around the organization took a very different approach to hiring for this role. Knowing this was a critical role and learning from their mistakes, the organization took a different approach to hiring. The individual that would replace him was well vetted among several other highly qualified candidates. He would come with the skill set and the capacity, as shown in his past experience, to succeed in the role. Additionally, the hiring process involved those he would be leading and supervising, therefore, giving a voice to the organization and ensuring a strong team fit.

Here the organization did their due diligence and hired a ten. In doing so, employee engagement improved, and employee turnover declined. Systems, efficiencies, and effectiveness improved, and this one critical hire got the organization back on track. It was a success story, and it was so because the organization took careful and thoughtful steps when hiring. **When we care for others, we do our due diligence to ensure we are surrounding them with good people.**

Love in Action

- When seeking to hire tens, what steps do you and/or your team take to ensure you are seeking the correct core competencies and aptitudes?

- What relational characteristics does your team find necessary to include in the job description? How will you ensure the candidate is a good fit for your team and employees?

- What type of mindset and/or dispositions are you seeking in a candidate? What type of person do you and your team want to work alongside?

- o In collaboration with your team, create a profile and/or job description for the type of person you are looking to hire. Use the questions above to help assist you in your thinking.

- What profile screeners (MBTI, Enneagram) do you use to select candidates and what type of results are you seeking?

  - o Research the type of interview screeners there are available in your industry and evaluate them to see if this approach may serve to help improve your hiring practices.

- In your interview process how do you uncover the genuine nature of your candidate and what interview experiences can you use to gain that understanding?

  - o Plan your interview process carefully. Examine how you can approach the process to capture a clear and genuine understanding of the candidate.

- What industry specific hiring tools can you use to find high-quality talent? Are there networks you can tap into that will help you fish the right streams?

  - o Get involved with a human resource network. Learn from others inside or outside of your industry as to where to fish and find the right candidates.

Chapter

Teams on Target with Tools

Give people more control and they will thrive.

—*Dr. Henry Cloud*

To summarize so far, we have spent our time focused on leading ourselves and others with love and care. We know the importance of loving ourselves and developing the habits and routines of self-care that lead us to personal edification. When we enter our leadership arena as complete persons, filled with meaning and purpose, steeped in healthy personal routines, we are positioned to be able to care and love those we are leading. In doing so, we strive to set up an organizational climate that supports teamwork, mentorship, and the habits, rituals, and routines of organizational well-being. In chapter 10, we will continue to share and express our care by developing the supporting systems that will lead to organizational effectiveness and team success.

To highlight Dr. Cloud's quote above: *If we give people control, they will thrive*. As leaders, providing our people with autonomy will lead to greater ownership and success in their work. When providing autonomy, however, we must also collaborate to develop the appropriate structures and systems in which to operate. Developing appropriate boundaries and structures will allow your people to operate freely within the organization while keeping your teams on target.

A colleague of mine was leading a mid-sized organization. This organization was a little over 120 employees and included approximately ten different departments. When he took over the organization, it had been suffering from a culture and climate crisis largely due to a derogatory top-down management approach. Employees felt disengaged and very unappreciated. Teams were operating in silos and any progress that was made in one team was poorly communicated to the rest of the organization, therefore, leaving little lasting impact. This particular company lacked the components of organizational well-being and organizational structure, leaving the potential effectiveness of a great group of people untapped.

He began to tackle these challenges by getting a clear understanding of the issues that were being faced. He set up department focus groups to gather information about the issues and sought first to understand their viewpoints. He asked probing questions and sought to unpack the root causes of employee disengagement and organizational ineffectiveness. After spending the first sixty days meeting with employees and unpacking their growth *opportunities*, he began to collaboratively develop a plan for greater organizational effectiveness and employee well-being.

(Take note of the word opportunities used in the last sentence. The way we use language and how we frame our challenges are important. The use of language in many ways creates our realities. He chose to frame his challenges as opportunities in order to respect the work that was already being done within the organization. He chose the word opportunities because he wanted to let those he was now leading know that he valued and respected the work they had been doing. Their efforts were valued and together they were going to capitalize on their opportunities for growth and improvement. On the contrary, I have seen other leaders come into similar situations

and tell people how they were doing it all wrong and that the savior was now here to help them overcome their poor performance. Using negative language or blame such as this causes the fight-or-flight mechanism in our brains to fire, leading to employee protectionism and lack of trust. Bottom line, choose your words carefully and respect people's hard work. It pays dividends!)

Back to the story. After gathering a clear picture of the organization and understanding the challenges that they were facing, my colleague began to intentionally design a system that would promote employee involvement, engagement, shared decisions making, teamwork and collaboration. To start, he developed an advisory council that included the leaders of each department. With department leaders at table, he began to ask some defining questions:

- How did they want to do business together as a team?
- How did this team envision this organization operating at its fullest potential?
- What was the meaning and purpose of their work?
- How do they establish trust among one another?
- What were the norms and commitments they should develop as a team?
- How do they identify and execute their goals and objectives?
- How do they design their standard operating procedures?

And while there were many long conversations and many more questions, he began to till the soil for developing an organization that had a purpose. He was preparing his advisory council to design a business that was intentionally structured for employee well-being, engagement, and organizational effectiveness.

As the advisory council continued to meet and design the systems and principles that would guide their work together, their starting point included developing team norms and commitments. Once they were able to agree upon how they would operate as a team and what they were willing to commit to, the team was able to move forward with developing their goals, objectives and actions plans. Further, the advisory council began to develop long term organizational protocols and systems for dealing with future opportunities and change. I share this story because it illustrates how my colleague was able to turn around an organization by developing teams who were on target with tools.

In this chapters, we will look at:

- The Three Ts: Teams on target with tools. Developing a healthy, collaborative environment of reciprocal accountability with a rhythm of consistency; the ability to cooperate, to support shared decision-making and creativity while also employing intentional tools that keep the team and the organization moving forward.

Teams on Target with Tools

- **Teams:** Designing our organizations into teams allows for the management of people and workflow. When we lead with love, we are driven to ensure that we create the right environment for teams to thrive and engage.

- **On Target:** Cohesive teams that are positioned for success have a clear understanding of their why, their goals and their objectives. They clearly understand what success looks like and are focused on desired outcomes.

- **Tools:** In order for strong, cohesive teams to exist and remain on target, they must be equipped with the right tools. Teams must utilize the correct organizational structures and protocols that will allow them to flourish.

Team Development

Developing Teams and Team Norms

When we approach our work with the best intentions, we do so because we care about the people we work with and the accomplishments we are trying to achieve. It is our intention to achieve our goals and to provide a meaningful and fulfilling working experience along the way. To that end, it is necessary to establish the rules of engagement with our team and the larger organization. It is through the development and adherence to organizational norms that we develop a cohesive organizational culture. As teams, if we expect to operate effectively, we must agree upon a clearly defined set of behaviors. Establishing norms of behavior allows the members of the organization to understand what we have agreed upon and how we have decided to operate together.

Much like we discussed in chapter 6, work is a social exchange. It is an agreement among members to balance a give-and-take within our operating system. Employers provide payment; employees provide their time. Employers create meaningful and engaging work; employees give more of their hearts and minds and take ownership of the success of the organization. This quid pro quo, if you will, allows for the work to take place and outcomes to be achieved. When we lead with love, it is important to consider how this social exchange will take place from a psychological and behavioral perspective—that is, we must consider how we plan to behave with one another in order to create a meaningful and engaging environment. The greatest teams and organizations always have a way of doing business.

Establishing team and organizational norms is much like building a fence for your team. Much like a fence for your yard, which is purposed for keeping certain things in and others out, team norms are similar, in that they are designed to keep the right behavior inside the team while keeping the wrong behaviors out. It is for this purpose that we develop team norms to establish principles and boundaries that give us a clear focus, support the social emotional well-being of our people, foster our shared beliefs about our work, and establish the rules of engagement allowing us to operate succinctly.

A brief illustration here, and you can certainly read more about this on your own: Executive functioning is the brain's basic operating system for achieving any specific outcome or activity. Executive functioning skills allow us to focus on 1) the things we should be intentionally doing, 2) the things we should be intentionally avoiding, and 3) working memory, which is the brain's ability to store and process information for decision-making. Much like the brain's executive functioning system, is the need to develop organizational norms. The organization must decide upon what behaviors will be intentionally practiced, what behaviors will be intentionally avoided, and how it will use its collective skills to achieve its outcomes.

When establishing norms, we should start by asking some basic questions that will guide our work together and allow for more effective decision-making and workflow.

Structuring Time

When we establish team or organizational norms, we want to start by establishing the expectations around our time frames and how we respect our time together. While organizational norms and behaviors vary, and some organizations may be loose with meeting times and how meetings and teams operate, you will want to consider how you want to use and manage your time. As the leader, you will want to establish clarity around your meeting times.

- **Will weekly, biweekly, monthly, or quarterly meetings allow you to reach your goals?** You must understand what you need to accomplish and how often you need to meet to do so.

- **Will your meeting times adhere to a start and end time? Is there diligent adherence to these start and end times?** How you manage this will impact efficiencies and effectiveness. It also shows respect for people's time. It should be noted here that there are undoubtedly cultural nuances to management of time. How you and your team establish your rules around time should take into consideration your cultural norms as well as the importance you place on your time together for achieving outcomes.

- **Will meetings require punctuality?** Meaning, does your team expect things to start on time? Some teams are loose, and others are tight on such norms. For you and your team, you will want to decide on these questions so that everyone is aware of the expectation. Respect for team norms can break down when one person walks in five minutes late to each meeting.

Determining Confidentiality

As you work to develop a cohesive team, the expectation around confidentiality must be clear and well understood. I have witnessed teams take some serious hits when there was a lack of clarification around confidentiality issues, so spending some time to solidify the processes and expectations for releasing information is a must.

- **What information is embargoed and what is available for release?** As a team it should be clear what information is allowed to be shared with others in the organization and what information should be strictly held in confidence among team members.

- **Allow or not to allow parking-lot meetings?** Establishing some open and honest expectations around what can be said after the formal meeting has ended is necessary. This can be tricky. Oftentimes smaller meetings take place outside the larger group for the purpose of planning, gaining consensus, and so forth. And while this can be a perfectly natural way of operating, it may have some implications related to confidentiality and team cohesiveness. Being clear on what can be discussed after the meeting is imperative. Some outside meetings are often referred to as parking-lot meetings. Meaning, metaphorically, they take place after the primary meeting, in the parking lot, where people share how they really feel about what happened in the meeting. They may share their discontent or their frustrations or their lack of agreement on an issue that was discussed. In order to keep dissent from taking place in the parking lot, however, we have to be clear about our expectations, and we must maintain an honest and open meeting space, where people are free to share ideas safely. If we can provide people with an honest, open, and safe place to contribute to the team, fewer parking-lot conversations will take place. Setting clear expectations about parking-lot conversation is important and ensures that people can be open and honest and will help support cohesive and confidential communications.

Listening and Participation

As you and your team design your expectations and norms you will want to consider how you approach listening and participation. Oftentimes these patterns develop naturally with professional teammates, but setting boundaries does not hurt to solidify your practices.

- **Who has the floor?** Setting clear expectations around who will speak and how you will handle interruptions can be necessary. Having well planned agendas can assist with this. For example, agendas can be designed to give specific members or department reps of your team an opportunity to contribute at a specific point in the meeting. This can be easy if the meeting is a debrief or informational. But if this is a problem-solving committee, which requires back and forth discussion, you will want to set up norms for who has the floor and how you transition from one member to another. There are lots of simple, fun, and creative ways to approach this that can add some light to a meeting. You need to find what is good for your team and your culture when designing these norms.

- **How will your team manage participation?** As teams come together, conversations about participation and engagement may be necessary. Great teams are marked by their ability to concentrate and focus. Setting up the guidelines for how people will participate and how they will maintain focus is necessary in keeping teams on task and moving toward their goals.

- **How will you and your team manage distractions?** Teams are often charged with multiple tasks and projects. In developing your norms, it will be important to set guidelines for staying on task and managing distractions so that projects and topics do not overlap or remain incomplete. How teams will be brought back to focus and remain on target must be established. You can do this by managing the conversation with timers, hand gestures and or even some fun or playful routines. Years back I worked on a newly developed team that was regularly off task. After a few weeks, it became obvious that the distractions were leading us to inefficiencies. We began to simply use a goofy little hand gesture (index finger to nose) when we would get off task. It was polite and lighthearted, but it allowed us to get back on track.

How Teams Make Decisions

How you design your team norms around decision-making will be critical to the effectiveness and success of your team. Team dynamics around decision-making can come in many forms. The variations in which organizations are formed and the way decisions are made can be endless. The intricacies of decision-making can be quite complex from both a technical and relational perspective. While this is not intended to be an exhaustive narrative about the infinite ways an organization can make decisions, I will pose a few questions here that are important to normative decision-making development.

- **Why does this team exist?** First, we must start by asking ourselves what type of decision-making body is this team? Is this team an advisory board or is this team tasked with completing action plans? Maybe this team is purposed for creativity or innovation. Whatever the purpose may be, the team must have decided and understand why it exists.

- **Who manages the team?** Teams are often led or managed in some form or fashion. Your team must decide who will be the leader or the manager when your team is together. While a hierarchy may exist in your organization, as it does in many, it should be understood that, at times, various members of a team may take the role of leader or manager. Being clear about who is leading or managing a team meeting will allow for greater clarity and cohesion.

- **Who is the expert in this matter?** When your team is involved in the decision-making process it can be helpful to clarify who are the leading experts on the team. Teams that include members with various skill sets and backgrounds will want to clarify who is positioned for providing the soundest advice and knowledge on any specific subject matter. Some teams come together with members from across an organization who are not in position to lead or give expert advice on one matter or another. Ensuring that your expert voices are elevated assists in establishing the importance of knowledgeable, expert-based decision-making.

- **How will your team deal with disagreement and build consensus?** Depending on the purpose of the team, the team may be in a position to make decisions that require consensus. With consensus can also come disagreement. Establishing team norms as to how you will make decisions can help alleviate any lack of clarity. For example, some teams or organizations may require a democratic process or even further, a legal process. Other teams may simply need a collaborative discussion led by a team leader who may make the final decision. There are many ways to build consensus and deal with disagreement and each team will have to navigate these challenges in accordance with their culture and expectations. Ray Dalio uses an interesting way of gathering consensus and making decisions by using what he calls the <u>Dot Collector.</u>[46] You can google Ray's dot collector and find out more about it.

Designing team norms and expectations creates a strong set of behavioral boundaries that allows team mates to understand the rules of engagement. Teams are more successful when they operate succinctly with behavioral discipline. And while developing norms and boundaries may seem restrictive by their very nature they are actually a source of freedom for you and your team. Because you have been intentional about how you choose to work together you no longer have to operate from a place of uncertainty. When rules, expectations, norms, and boundaries are set, there are increased efficiencies and no wasting time trying to figure out how to use your time, how to make decisions, and who is taking the lead. The planning of norms allows you to operate

---

[46]https://www.youtube.com/watch?v=vcQ1ELhyQKE

freely with clear understanding and teams are no longer tied down with uncertainty.

Designing strong teams takes intentionality and establishing the rules of engagement will assist in keeping your team on target. Designing the tools to keep your team on target should begin with setting the agenda, designing action plans, and building structural protocols.

On Target with Tools

Set Your Agenda

Like the captain of any ship, you must have a map to help guide you along your voyage. A map allows you to see both your start and end point. Well-designed teams, who have well designed norms, and who operated succinctly start their meetings with a clear and well-planned agenda. The agenda serves as a tool that keeps all members of your team informed and moving toward an end goal. Well planned agendas include:

- **Norms:** As mentioned above, agendas should include the norms that the team has agreed to adhere to. The norms should be visible and linked to the agenda. Norms should be reviewed on a regular basis to keep people aware and on track.

- **Purpose:** Agendas should tend to the purpose of the meeting. Essentially, the agenda should answer up front the question: Why are we meeting?

- **Goals and Objectives:** Once we know our purpose, a well-planned agenda should include the goals and the objectives. In other words, what should be the outcome achieved by the end of the meeting?

- **Action items:** Agendas should also capture the action items discussed within the meeting with specific clarity. When a meeting has concluded, each team member must understand the tasks they are to complete and the dates and expectations for delivery.

- **Leaderships roles:** In many cases, agendas may need to include leadership role expectations. Meaning, as mentioned above, that specific members of the teams need to have it made clear that they are leading the agenda at a specific time or covering a specific portion of the agenda. For example, in a director-level meeting, the agenda should specify when the human resources director will lead, when the marketing director will lead, then the operations director, and so forth.

- **Record of minutes:** Agendas should include a record of the minutes. Minutes may simply capture a record of topics discussed, all action items and persons responsible for completing those action items.

- **Habits of well-being:** When we lead with love, let us not forget the habits, rituals, and routines that support a thriving team. Agendas should and must include leaving time and space for human connection, fun, gratitude, celebration, and appreciation. The heart must always be included in the agenda!

Teams on Target Use Action Plans

Keeping teams focused and on target not only requires agendas but also a plan of attack for those things we set out to accomplish together. This is where the action plan comes into account. Action plans are simple tools that drive intentionality and keep teams moving in the right direction. They allow each team member to understand the goals, objectives, who is responsible for which task, and completion dates. Action plans are not rocket science, unless, of course, they are for making rockets. Sorry, I digress, but they are a necessity. Too often teams operate without clear direction and without clear and concise action plans, which leads to unnecessary confusion and undisciplined workflow.

Action plans are simple and can take many forms depending on the nature of the organization. Below is an elementary template for action planning:

10.1 Action Plan Template

Goal: The aligned goal to the mission and vision of the organization.					
Objective: The task to be completed that will support the goal	**Person Responsible:** Assigns the task to the individual(s)	**Progress Update:** Date(s) for progress inspection	**Completion Date:** Date of expected completion	**Persons Involved:** List of people who are responsible for executing the action plan and monitoring its progress	**Notes:** Additional information that may be useful to the implementation of the action plan
Notable Constraints: Forces that are working for or against the progress of the actions plan.					
Conclusion and Communication: Once this action plan is complete it should be decided how the plans completion will be shared and with whom.					
What's next?: Next steps, next action plan, next meeting.					

Actions plans can take many forms, and organizations use many variations to accomplish their goals and objectives. Action plans can be very simple or more complex than described here. At their foundation, they are to be used to intentionally coordinate your team's effort for a *purpose*—that is, our team must know that the action plan houses a purpose for our actions and what we are setting out to accomplish. Further, action plans solidify our expected *results.* This allows teams to know the exact expectations, for a specific task, with explicit time constraints. Finally, action plans are in themselves, action. They are the roadmap for success. They let the team see what is being done, why it is being done, who is responsible for accomplishing the task and when it will be accomplished. Along the way, action plans provide for progress monitoring to ensure you are on target, and, if not, teams can adjust the plan accordingly.

To paraphrase thought leader Jim Collins in *Good to Great*:[47] Successful organizations include disciplined people, disciplined

---

[47]Jim Collins, *Good to Great: Why Some Companies Make the Leap ... and Others Don't* (New York: HarperCollins, 2009), 102–105.

thought, and disciplined action. Action plans are tools that drive disciplined people, disciplined thought and action, and the development of action plans leads to successful and intentional outcomes. Leading with love requires us to be thoughtful and intentional with those we lead and creating clear action plans with our teams allows them to operate clearly, succinctly, and effectively.

Teams on Target Keeping Score: Lead and Lag Measures

When developing action plans thought must be given to the performance drivers that will impact the success of reaching our intended goal. Prior to the achievement of a goal comes the performance of a set of tasks that directly impact the achievement of that specific goal. The antecedents, or the actions that come before reaching a goal can be referred to as the lead measures. A lead measure is an action item, a step in a process, or a task that impacts the lag measure. The lag measure is the intended outcome which is trying to be achieved.[48]

To make this simple, let me share an example. I have a friend and colleague who impressively completed an Ironman competition which includes a 2.5-mile swim, 26.2-mile run (marathon), and a 100-mile bike ride. This is an enormous feat of strength and endurance. In this example the Lag Measure is the completion of the Iron Man. Essentially that was her goal—to complete the task. Now, before she ever began the Ironman competition there was a year's worth of training that took place to prepare. The training schedule she kept could be referred to as her lead measures. Simply put, the completion of her lead measures allowed her to reach her goal—that is, her lag measure. In order to reach her goal, she had to keep to a strict training regimen, which included daily training sessions dedicated to swimming, biking, and running. Along the way, she kept score. Much like golfers keep score on each and every hole (lead) to come to a cumulative score at the end (lag), she kept score, or a record, of every daily workout task. Very simply, the scorecard may have looked a little like this:

---

[48]Chris McChesney, Sean Covey, and Jim Huling, *The 4 Disciplines of Execution: Achieving Your Wildly Important Goals* (New York: Simon and Schuster, 2012).

10.2 Lead and Lag Measure Scorecard

Measures	Day 1 Lead Measure	Day 2 Lead Measure	Day 3 Lead Measure	Day 4–300 Lead Measures	Lag Measure
Task	Run 4 miles Bike 25 miles Swim 1 mile	Run 8 miles Bike 50 miles Swim 2 miles	Run 2 mile Bike 12 miles Swim .5 miles	Continued ... You get the gist	Complete the Ironman Competition
Completed	2 hours	4 hours	1 hour	X	16 hours

This is an oversimplified example, but you catch the drift. Each lead measure is intended to assist in accomplishing the intended goal or Lag measure. Along the way the score is being kept in either hours or status of completion.

Another example might include something along these lines: In many industries employee safety is a daily issue. Ensuring workplace safety and eliminating workplace injuries can save organizations significant time and money.

In order to do so, organizations will put forth lead measures that will impact their over goals (lag measure) to decrease workplace injuries. Here is another brief example of what that may look like:

10.3 Lead and lag Measure Scorecard

Measures	Lead Measure	Lead Measure	Lead Measure	Lead Measures	Lag Measure
Task	Weekly Safety Meetings to review procedures	Individual production Station Safety checklists	Clear and appropriated directions and signage at each production station	Weekly reward and incentive plan for zero workplace injuries	Annually decrease lost days due to injury by 300 percent
Completed	X	X	X	X	16 hours

In this example, there are several lead measures put in place that are intended to impact the overall lag measure defined as: Decreasing days lost to injury by 300 percent. Here the organization intends to have weekly meetings to remind and review workplace safety procedures and protocols. Additionally, the organization has put in place the individual safety checklist at each production station that requires the employee to review and check completion on a daily basis. Further, the organization put in place appropriate signage and communications to direct and inform employees of necessary safety protocols. Finally, they put in place a weekly reward incentive to celebrate their successes along the way. This is a very simple and very real example that has been shared with me from a consultant I recently interviewed. When we lead with intention, using our scorecard to document our lead and lag measures can help us chart our course and stay accountable to our progress. Great leaders are specific about where they are taking their team and they can show them the roadmap to get there.

Teams on Target Use Protocols to Uncover Truth and Root Causes

Leading with love often requires us to face truth and reality in order to be able to move our teams and organizations in the right direction. When we care deeply about our people and our achievements together, it is imperative that we design a playbook and use protocols that allow us to operate with truth and transparency. At times, teams may operate on incorrect information outside the lines of what is real and true within their organization, which can often lead to poor and off target performance. I have witnessed this on many occasions in which leaders have not created a culture of trust and have not utilized appropriate collaborative tools to uncover a true reality. This has led to organizational confusion and poor execution. To paraphrase the astronaut Scott Kelly: "None of us is as dumb as all of us." Meaning that oftentimes groupthink or fear of repercussion from our superiors leads to silence, compliance, or the inability for people to share the truth about a situation. This can be extremely dangerous.

Let me ask: Have you witnessed a time when a team has agreed to a bad decision? Have you been involved when a team is not willing to point out the errors in the boss's thinking? Have you been a part of a team that has gone in the wrong direction because they are not operating on correct information? I have. And in order to prevent those situations to the best of our ability, we must put in place behavioral practices—that is, questions and protocols—that help us to uncover truth and to operate transparently.

One tool that may be used is what I refer to as the "For Us, Against Us Protocol." This protocol is designed to walk teams through a process of uncovering truth and reality. It allows participants to define the challenges they are facing, identify potential causes within and outside their control, and develop a vision of what it would look like if the problem were solved. Further, this tool intends to assist teams in seeing what areas of their efforts are working for them and what areas are working against them. Uncovering their effective efforts and tossing aside their ineffective efforts allows teams to operate with a more concentrated focus on those things that are leading to their success. Utilizing a series of questions—that is, protocols—allows us to be focused and truthful in our approach to uncovering work that is focused and effective.

For Us or Against Us Protocol

This protocol is designed to assist participants in addressing challenging issues utilizing executive functioning that relates to understanding, self-regulation, and problem-solving.

10.4 For Us or Against Us Protocol

Define the Problem: What is the challenge you or your organization are facing?	
Notes:	

Potential causes for the challenge?	
Inside your control:	*Outside your control:*
Notes:	*Notes:*

What would it look like if the challenge were solved?	
Notes:	

What are we doing that is working for us?	*What are we doing that is working against us?*
Notes:	*Notes:*

Action Plan: Describe tangible actions that can be taken to solve the issue. Include the who/what/how it will be measured:	
Notes:	

The For Us, Against Us Protocol is an example of a simple tool that can lead to truth and transparency in decision-making. As effective leaders, it is our role to research and design protocols that lead us to uncovering our own truth and reality. Operating with truth and understanding the root causes of our success and failures positions us for success.

Teams on Target Design Tools and Protocols

Effective leaders, and those of us seeking to create the right culture and conditions for success, understand there are tools that will support us and our teams. Teams that have the right players, who are driven for success, utilize tools to assist them in uncovering truth and plan their actions. While agendas keep teams focused on the goals and objectives, action plans keep teams working in tandem to maximize efficiency. Effective leaders also utilize scorecards for lead and lag measures allowing teams to target their goals, monitor their progress, and calibrate for success. Designing and utilizing protocols and tools is a key element in keeping teams moving forward and focused. As leaders, we must do the research to design specific tools and protocols for our teams.

Although this is not intended to be a lesson on all the possible tools that support your specific organization there are many tools available that can assist with:

- Problem-solving
- Workflow
- Project management
- Systems management
- Employee culture and engagement
- Process designs and mapping
- Organizational systems and systemics
- Mental models

I recommend researching tools and protocols related to your specific industry. Further, for more on this topic, I recommend researching the Lean Six Sigma processes for additional protocols and design measures. Also, I would suggest researching Jim Collins, author of many great books on organizational success and design, along with Ray Dalio, author of *Principles*.

Summary

There is no shortage of research on the tools and protocols that could potentially assist you and your team in becoming a more connected and effective team. Most importantly is the understanding that in order for us and our teams to be effective we have to be highly intentional about how we operate. How we meet and manage our time should be well planned and coordinated. **The organizational culture that exists within our teams should not occur by default, but by design.** We must collaboratively craft our team's organizational norms of behavior and adhere to our commitments. When our norms guide our behaviors, we operate with boundaries allowing us to be focused and effective in our actions. Each team member understands their role and how to operate as a team member.

Further, when norms are firmly established, teams can focus on the targets—namely, goals and objectives—they are designed to achieve. Tools such as agendas and action plans support team direction and ensure teams are operating effectively and efficiently. When teams are working in harmony, with a clear focus on their targets, and with the tools and protocols to plan and execute their objectives, they are in a position to reach their goals and achieve success.

Leading with love means being intentional about creating teams that are on target with the supporting tools for successful outcomes.

Love in Action

- How do your teams operate? Are team and organizational culture intentionally created through behavioral norms?

- As a leader, what type of team culture have you intentionally designed?

- Are there clear and specific norms of behavior that have been designed and agreed upon?

- o With your team, design your team norms. Use the questions listed in this chapter to intentionally design your team, your team behavior, and your team's commitments to one another.

- How is team time used? What tools—that is, agendas, action plans, or other problem-solving and process tools—are being used to keep people moving forward in achieving their goals?

- What types of tools will you bring to your team that will allow them to be able to better reach their goals and objectives? Are you tracking your lead and lag measures?

- There are many tools for action planning, project management, etc. Determining which tools work for you and your team and make them a regular part of your rhythm of consistency to hit your targets.

Chapter

Aerial Perspective for Change Management

Observe constantly that all things take place by change,
and accustom thyself to consider that the nature of the Universe
loves nothing so much as to change the things which are,
and to make new things like them.

—*Marcus Aurelius*

Bringing the right members aboard our ship, setting the table for connection, and giving them the right tools, supports a team in their drive to succeed and achieve. And while the ship is sailing at sea it will often come in contact with storms that necessitate a change in course or adjustment of the sails. Change in direction and course corrections are inevitable. All things change, and in order to meet those changes with composure and adaptability we need to make use of the tools that will support our ability to adjust to an ever-changing environment.

In 2020 the United States and the global economy took a major hit due to the COVID-19 pandemic, which shuttered people indoors, causing businesses and organizations across the country to operate differently. Small businesses, the travel and leisure industry, and bars and restaurants, just to name a few, were decimated by the pandemic as people were no longer able to congregate or occupy indoor spaces together. With people staying home and limiting their travel, businesses had to rethink how they operated and had to make some significant changes just in order to survive.

A colleague of mine was a small business owner at the time whose small retail shop relied heavily on foot traffic. The quaint little shop was positioned in a prime location and passersby would stop in to buy unique clothing, jewelry, and other cool little accessories. With the city on lockdown and business struggling, she had to adapt and change in order to keep the doors open, her staff employed and herself in business.

In order to do so, she has to look at the overall business environment with which she was working. The environment had changed. She had far less foot traffic and fewer visitors coming through her doors during the height of the pandemic. This meant fewer people who would be browsing the merchandise and potentially purchasing products. The business model she had counted on for years was no longer going to work!

Further, she recognized that the culture of her organization was one of friendly, in-person customer service. She relied heavily on the charm and skill set of her salespeople on the floor to assist customers and support sales. With few visitors, her quaint and cozy culture was not serving to support sales. She knew something had to change if she were to stay afloat.

As the pandemic lingered on month after month she realized she needed to bring her product and her company's charm to the customers who were no longer coming in, but who were now sitting at home shopping online. In order to do so, she needed some new competencies and skills to be able to market and promote her product and her company culture in the online environment. Being able to survive in this new business environment meant that she needed to be able to expand her marketing skills and her knowledge of the online sales environment to be able to better reach her customers. That is the exact direction she took. She moved to update her skills and capacities by partnering with other experts in on-line sales and moved to market her products and her charm online. As her online presence grew through social media and other outlets, she was able to improve her sales and keep things afloat.

The story doesn't end here, though. Not only did she adapt to the business environment but she was also able to build capacity among herself and her employees to be able to reach a customer base she had not tapped into in the past. Her new online marketing strategy would outlive the COVID-19 pandemic and position her for greater sales and success down the road.

As organizational leaders, it is important for us to be able to change and adapt to our environment. In doing so, we oftentimes have to step back and examine our situation from an aerial view—that is, we need to get above our situation and examine it in its entirety. This includes us looking at the environment, our culture, our conditions, and our competencies and skill sets.

Take an Aerial View

Examining our own organizational environment relies on our perspective, and oftentimes it requires us to look down at our challenges from atop. Seeing things from an aerial view allows us to examine complex organizational challenges in their entirety. As leaders, oftentimes we may be too close to our organizational challenges, and we may be unable to see them for what they are. You may be aware of the old *Standing too close to the Elephant* parable. The idea is simply this: sometimes we stand too close to something, which actually disrupts seeing that thing in its entirety. By standing too close, we are not able to understand the entire picture, much like the cartoon below illustrates. Only by stepping back from the elephant do we see the entire animal.

The notion is similar in our own organizations. Only when we can take an aerial view of the environmental landscape can we begin to see our reality in its entirety. When we are able to take such a view and see our organizational challenges in their entirety, we are then in a position to gain more knowledge, information and understanding about our challenges and/or our reason for success.

When seeking a new perspective through our aerial positioning there are both practical and tactical approaches that we can take to examine our current reality. An aerial perspective allows us to survey the landscape and determine if we have either technical challenges or behavioral deficits or both.

Identify Technical Challenges

Technical challenges are those that are largely logistic or systemic. They are systems challenges that can often be remedied with technical solutions. Technical challenges may come in an infinite number of ways depending on the industry. A simple example may include process disruptions. Many industries rely heavily on efficient processes to keep them moving forward, and when there are disruptions in the process they may find themselves leaking revenue. In order to get the company back up and running, the process disruption must be solved and then the company is back to profitability. For many process-related companies, reducing the number of disruptions to their process is critical and would be considered a technical challenge.

During the summers when I was in my undergraduate program, I worked as a painter. While doing so, one of the jobs I was tossed on was at a food packaging facility. Being in my teens I was fascinated by the mechanics of the packaging plant and the intricacies of the process. The machinery was enormous, and it seemed like a maze of belts, rollers, and robots. As I was working to paint the boundary lines on the floor in bright yellow paint, I would regularly hear a loud alarm and see the large packaging machine come to a halt. I was curious as to why the line was being stopped so often. One of the managers was walking past at the time and I asked what was causing the stoppage. He simply explained that the belts on the system would get loose on a regular basis, or the bagging process would get jammed. This seemed to me a bit foolish to have a system requiring constant maintenance and regular stoppages. But no one asked me, and I continued painting my lines.

This was, however, a classic case of a technical challenge. The process would be more efficient, and less time would be lost if the company was able to fix their technical problem and reduce the number of stoppages. Organizational leaders who take an aerial view and seek to improve their process know the importance of identifying technical challenges and seeking their resolution. Technical challenges can be truly challenging and may take the cooperation of many people in order to solve, but they are oftentimes identifiable and with cooperative effort, solvable. Beyond technical problems, however, often lies behavioral issues, which also require an aerial perspective to allow for complete examination. As leaders, it is important that we gain perspective to be able to decipher between the two.

Identify Behavioral Challenges

In chapter 10, I touched on an example of workplace safety where action planning served to improve the safety condition for the workplace. The example used in chapter 10 focused largely on changing the behaviors of employees. This is not to say that there are not technical elements related to workplace safety, there certainly are. However, the example used in chapter 10 sought to change worker behaviors by utilizing specific tools such as weekly meetings, signage, and safety incentives. From your own experience, you may even recall stories in which some companies prominently display the number of days without workplace injuries so as to keep people keenly aware of the importance of safety.

When we take an aerial perspective and seek to improve our organizations it is important that we recognize the importance of behavioral change. Behaviors are fueled by habits, mindsets, knowledge, and incentives. In order to improve or change, understanding the behaviors that lead to our outcomes is important. Again, let's go back to the safety example in chapter 10.

In an effort to decrease the number of workplace injuries, the management sought to implement an action plan that changed the behaviors of the employees by imparting their daily routines, increasing their awareness of the safety issues and incentivizing behavior.

You may recall, one of the lead measures within the action plan included conducting weekly safety meetings. These meetings were designed to increase knowledge and understanding of safety related issues. The weekly meetings were routine and brought safety to the forefront of the minds of both the employees and the management. In conducting these regular meetings management sought to impact the mindset, awareness and understanding of the importance of workplace safety for the purpose of changing employees' behaviors.

Beyond the weekly safety meetings, you may remember the addition of safety checklists. These checklists were a tool designed to take employees through a series of safety steps prior to operating their machines. The checklist tool served as a mechanism for changing behavior. This tool directed employees to be keenly aware of their surroundings, and the necessary safety precautions related to their machines. Again, this tool was designed for behavioral change. It creates an intentional awareness of the necessary safety precautions for the operation of their machines.

In addition to weekly meetings and safety checklists, the leaders of the organization added safety signage to bring further awareness to the issue of workplace safety. Again, another measure designed to impact the behavior of employees and decrease workplace injury.

Finally, it was mentioned that there was a weekly reward and incentive plan instituted to provide motivation for reduced workplace injuries. Economic rewards and incentives are often used to change behaviors and promote desired outcomes. In this example, the reward or incentive may be that of additional bonus pay, time off, or other rewards deemed valuable to the employee. I have often seen bonus pay and financial rewards spur increased desired behavior, but there are certainly other rewards that are seen as valuable. The important element of incentivization is that the reward is deemed valuable by the employee and that it is used wisely so as to not be considered unattainable, overly competitive, or that it serves to actually disincentivize. Just a word of caution: Be thoughtful and careful with incentivization plans. If not done with wisdom, they can backfire and actually demotivate individuals.

As we can see, when we are seeking to manage change and examine our current reality, it is vital to get above the issues and determine if they are technical, behavioral, or both. In order to properly understand our challenges, it is absolutely imperative that we assess our situation accurately, to the best extent possible, so that we are able to operate on correct information. If we manage change without accurate information, we position ourselves to make poor decisions, which can have potentially negative consequences.

Cultural Aspects of Change

When we recognize a need to change or adapt, it is important to take an aerial view to gain an understanding or our organizational culture. I appreciate Tony Wager's definition of organizational culture as it refers to the shared values, beliefs, assumptions, expectations, and behaviors along with the mindsets that permeate an organizational system.[49] Gathering an understanding of our

[49]Wagner, Tony, Robert Kegan, Lisa Laskow Lahey, Richard W. Lemons, Jude Garnier, Deborah Helsing, Annie Howell, and Harriette Thurber Rasmussen. *Change leadership: A practical guide to transforming our schools.* John Wiley & Sons, 2012.

organization's strengths and weaknesses requires us to uncover some of the underlying beliefs, mindset and behaviors that often exist by default rather than intentionality. **When we lead with love, we do so with intentionality, and we must pay close attention to the underlying culture upon which our organization operates.**

In 2020, during the COVID-19 pandemic, companies, schools, and churches were all forced to rethink the way they operated. They had to examine the underlying assumptions, beliefs, and mindsets about their organizations and determine how they were going to operate moving forward. Churches, for example, had to do a serious cultural examination of their operations in order to continue operating and providing the services that they had typically offered. One of the largest churches in the Chicagoland area had to examine its underlying mindsets and beliefs in order to keep its congregation intact. Let me share:

For years, one large suburban church relied on utilizing their over ten-thousand-seat arena to draw worshipers together for their Saturday and Sunday services. This church was beautifully designed, offered outstanding musical talent, and offered an engaging spiritual experience, along with a host of activities for kids, families, and many others. Recognizing that they were unable to perform many of the functions that draw churches together for fellowship and camaraderie they had to rethink and promote some new cultural beliefs and behaviors.

First, they had to be intentional about promoting the idea that church is not just about a building, or the music, or the beautiful venue. This was not an easy task for a church that relied so heavily on its facilities. Further, because they were not able to gather, they had to promote small group fellowship through online gatherings that had traditionally relied on close meetings over lunch and in the homes of worshipers. This church was forced to examine the underlying beliefs, mindsets, and values about what togetherness and fellowship truly meant. It forced them to rethink the true meaning of church. Togetherness could no longer be dependent upon their arena. They had to bring their worship services to each and every parishioner's living room through online virtual access. Along with their worship services, they also had to rethink how their small groups would stay intact and how they would manage their operations. Small group leaders would need to promote the importance of small group interaction while setting up a new online meeting platform to carry out small group work.

While this is a simple example of the cultural aspects of change, it is important to examine the underlying cultural issues that exist within your own organization. Understanding organizational culture allows for a more focused and clear change plan. You may want to ask: How do people behave? What do they assume about the organization and its operations? How do your assumptions lead to blind spots? What are the mindsets that exist within your organization?

If the culture of your organization needs examination or retooling, be sure that you're gathering correct information about your behavioral culture in order to provide an appropriate diagnose when planning for change.

Competencies and Skill Sets

As we continue to take an aerial view and examine our change management strategies it is also useful to examine our skill sets and competencies. As I mentioned above, as organizations across the globe had to adapt to the COVID-19 pandemic, one of the key elements that would lead to organizational success was the ability for individuals to adapt their skill sets to their new environments.

For example, as mentioned above, in churches, small group leaders would need to take their meetings online, and individuals would need to grow their skill sets in order to conduct online small group gatherings and teaching.

Educators across the country had to do the same. Teachers were forced to become online instructors overnight and they had to greatly increase their competencies for teaching students remotely from home.

Retailers, like the one mentioned above, had to adapt and move their products online and develop a system of online shopping and delivery as well.

These are just a few examples. When digging into your change management strategy, examining the skills and competencies you and your team may need is vital to success moving forward.

Conditions for Change: Time, Space, and Resources

While change may require examining the organizational culture or employee skills and competencies, it may also require aerial positioning to look at our conditions. Our conditions refer to how we utilize our time, our spaces, and our resources. When we are positioned for change, it is necessary to have a keen understanding of these conditions in order to accurately design a change strategy moving forward.

While many organizations have been forced to change over the years due to changes in the market or other environmental factors, they have had to consider how they use their time, space, and resources. You may recall when Walgreens moved to the "Corner of Happy and Healthy." They began moving their stores to corner locations to improve visibility and convenience. They used their spaces and resources differently to become more prominent and convenient.

After the 9/11 terrorist attacks, the Travel and Safety Administration had to adapt to keep air travel safe. They were forced to change and manage the way they used their resources and their spaces.

It doesn't stop there. There are countless examples of organizational change that have occurred in both the private and public sectors. Another example of adaptation due to conditional changes can be described during the COVID-19 pandemic, when restaurants and bars had to change their approach just to stay afloat. One restaurant conglomerate began moving its kitchens into industrial spaces just to be able to accommodate their pickup and delivery services. When the restaurant chain was available for dine-in, the kitchens had been designed to accommodate a specific number of guests. With people now eating at home, they have to accommodate for an additional *catering style* of business to replace their previous format. With the change in conditions, this restaurant group identified the necessity to change and adapted their approach to business.

More and more, as technology rapidly changes our lives and the way we operate, we must look at our conditions and determine how we need to adapt and adjust. In all areas—technology, agriculture, medicine, education, banking, and beyond—the conditions are changing. As leaders we need to have in place a mindset of adaptability and an openness to be willing to examine our conditions and adjust to change.

Leading with love requires intentional actions and a steadfast mindset for caring for our people and our organization. **When we purposefully position ourselves to take an aerial view of our organizations, we are putting forth the efforts that will lead to positive change. Taking an aerial view allows us to look down on our current reality and determine if that reality requires us to adapt or change. It also allows us to examine the root causes of that reality and uncover the antecedents for our success or failure. Aerial positioning allows us to view our reality in both behavioral and technical terms and determine if there are changes necessary within those areas. It also allows us to determine what, if any, cultural related issues need to be addressed along with any additional competency or conditional issues. Adapting and managing changes requires perspective, an aerial perspective that is, that positions us to observe reality in a way that offers a complete view of the landscape and its intricacies.**

Tools for Change

In chapter 10, we discussed the concept of teams on target with tools (3T's). As we manage change, we must also carry the 3T's into our change management strategy. In order to manage change, we have to use our collective intellectual resources, along with our targeted focus, and our tools. A couple basic tools that are often used in change management are the continue, start, stop (C/S/S) protocol and the SWOT analysis. Sidenote here: there are truly limitless tools to manage change; however, these two simple tools are a great way to start when seeking to adapt, change, analyze, and grow your organization.

Continue, Start, Stop Protocol

With nearly every team I have led in the last decade, I have used the C/S/S protocol (see table 11.1 below) to reflect and add perspective to our change management strategy. This simple protocol, when done with openness, transparency, and the trust of a strong team, can lead to great insight. It allows for the identification of our strengths, weaknesses, and our areas of growth.

With one such organization I had worked with, the C/S/S protocol allowed us to completely rethink our system of collaboration and communication. After engaging in a C/S/S discussion we identified our communication weaknesses and determined that if we were able to make some shifts in our organizational chart and our workflow, we could remedy our disconnection and work more congruently to accomplish our goals. While this example is meant to be simple, and there were a lot of other planning sessions that went into that change plan, let there be no mistake, it was the C/S/S conversation that led to greater perspective, understanding, and positive change.

11.1 Continue, Start, Stop Protocol

Continue—Start—Stop Protocol		
Continue	**Start**	**Stop**
What actions or behaviors are we doing that lead to us reaching our goals and/or objectives?	What actions or behaviors should we start doing that will lead us to reaching our goals and/or objectives?	What actions or behaviors should we stop doing that are prohibiting us from reaching our goals and/or objectives?

Again, this protocol is a simple and effective tool designed to keep your team on target and moving forward with intentionality and effectiveness. Change management protocols such as this allow us to purposefully engage in discussion and gain new perspective and understanding. This protocol supports collaboration and leads to new insights; and if your team needs to adjust the protocol to meet your specific demand, well, then do it, and be creative. Make it your own. The tool is designed to be open ended and allow for input, divergent thinking, and open discussions. When done with fidelity, with a foundation of trust, it can lend to improved collaboration, outcomes, and team performance.

SWOT Analysis

Another useful tool for managing change is the SWOT analysis. This is a popular tool used in many organizations to unpack information and manage change. The SWOT analysis is, again, relatively simple, but requires trust and competency among those who are involved.

11.2 SWOT Analysis

Strengths	Weaknesses
• What do you do well? • What unique resources can you draw on? • What do others see as your strengths?	• Where could you improve? • Where do you have fewer resources than others? • What are others likely to see as a weakness?
Opportunities	**Threats**
• What opportunities are you open to? • What trends could you take advantage of? • How can you turn your strengths into opportunities?	• What threats could harm you? • What is your competition doing? • What threats do your weaknesses expose you to?

A SWOT analysis is yet another tool that can serve to keep your team on target with an intentional focus on change and improvement. This tool may, or may not serve all organizations, and can obviously be adjusted to fit a specific organizational need. The key points here are twofold: 1) use tools to keep your change plan moving forward, and 2) be intentional about asking the right questions to uncover your strengths, weaknesses, opportunities, and threats.

While the SWOT analysis and the C/S/S protocol are tools to examine our organizations and position us for change, there are certainly countless tools that may better suit your organizational needs. Again, I would also recommend the Lean Six Sigma pocket handbook[50]. This simple easy to read toolkit offers a plethora of ideas for managing change and improvement.

---

[50]Michael L. George, et al. *Lean Six Sigma Pocket Toolbook* (McGraw-Hill Professional Publishing, 2004).

Levers for Change—How Does Change Happen?

Markets adjust, cultures shift, and political landscapes change. Human history is a story of change and adaptation to cultures, knowledge, and economies. It is our jobs as leaders to care for our people and our organizations by staying ahead of the curve by adapting to the force of change. Let there be no mistake: Change can be hard, and it often takes a lot of intellectual and financial resources. But it is often necessary to ensure future success.

Do you remember the video rental store Blockbuster? Once worth over six billion. Maybe you remember their late fees—what they internally called "managed dissatisfaction." Well, if you don't remember them, that is because the once video giant got picked apart by video rental subscriptions, such as Netflix. They failed to adapt and change to the market and cultural forces of the day, and they are now nothing more than a memory. I may be wrong—there may be a few stores left.

Point being, change is necessary and often required. In addition to gaining the aerial perspective required in understanding our current reality, it is also important to use leverage to motivate and push forward our change plans. Change can be scary and hard, and it can often be difficult to promote; therefore it is necessary to bring data and information, accountability structures, and relational capital to the table in order to push change forward.

Start with Data

When we embark on any path toward change, it is important to begin by gathering the appropriate data or information to inform your change plan. Data can be quantitative or qualitative depending on the nature of your organization, but it must also be accurate. Like I mentioned above, Blockbuster became obsolete because they did not respect the data—that is, the changing cultural landscape induced by the internet and the dissatisfaction their customers had with their late-fee structures. Ignoring this very important information, from both a quantitative and qualitative perspective, left them stagnant and ultimately they were passed by.

Change plans must be informed by accurate data and that data should serve as our lever to motivate change. For example, in 2008, when the US economy faced a meltdown in part due to the housing bubble, banks were forced to change their lending behaviors. After the housing crash of 2008, the US government took a hard look at the subprime lending practices of banks, who were allowed to lend money to people who were under qualified to pay back their loans. The number of foreclosures, short sales and defaults went through the roof. Using this data, the banks were forced to adjust their lending practices to ensure more secure loans.

In 2020, during the COVID-19 pandemic, retailers used data to inform their change plans as well. Seeing that in-store sales had dropped drastically and online shopping had made drastic increases due to the shuttering of the general population, stores like Target and Walmart began online shopping with curbside pickup. As I write this, it is ubiquitous in Target to see employees shopping for customers whom will wait outside for the target employee to place the goods in their cars.

Again, it was retail *data* that drove the change. **Leveraging data is one of the key components to motivating change. In your own organization, as you mount your change plan be sure that you and your team are gathering accurate data and information to support your need to change. Use that data to determine how you might need to change.** Like Target and Walmart, use data to adapt and move forward. Let your data be the driving force.

Relationships

Relational quality is another key lever to any change plan. As we have covered in part II, building relational capital through trust, well-being, and mentorship serves to engage our team in the work we share. **Relational capital is, in many ways, the lifeblood of any organization in that it connects our teammates to each other and to the mission and/or purpose of the organization**. When relational capital is high, members of the organization are willing to give of themselves in order to see the team succeed. People are willing to do the hard work that is necessary to see the organization thrive. High relational capital indicates that there is a strong sense of trust, engagement, and connectedness within the organization and among its members. This capital will serve as leverage for any necessary change efforts.

In the early 2000s, I was working with a high-performing team that oversaw the work of approximately two hundred employees. The team was well informed and well equipped to get the *right* work done with effectiveness. With such a talented and highly prepared team one might have expected there to be little resistance to change. This was not the case, however. At the onset of our work, we had very little relational capital. I remember one conversation I had with one of our more respected employees, he explained to me that although he knew we were doing the right things and that our top executive was "smart," he felt that our leader cared more about his resume than the organization. He explained that it was common for employees to feel used as a stepping-stone for this leader's future aspirations. Because of that relational deficit we met resistance to some very commonsense change initiatives. Had this particular leader made more intentional investments in relationships within the organization we would have seen less resistance to change.

Several years later, that particular leader moved on, as expected, and an individual who had moved up within the organization took the top executive's chair. Having worked with, and among, the employees within the organization there was a well invested relational bank account, so to speak. With this relational capital the new executive was able to move change forward with less resistance. The trust and genuine connection among the leader and the employees were far greater, and you could feel it in the relational climate of the organization. It was palpable. People trusted the leader and felt a connection.

Change comes with its challenges. Each of these leaders had to face resistance to change. **But change is more easily managed with a strong sense of relational capital in the form of trust and connectedness. Strong relationships pay dividends and there are very few shortcuts to genuine human connection.** Like we discussed in part II, if we want to care for our people we have to tap into their hearts, their motives, and their ambitions. We have to provide opportunities for genuine connections and well-being.

Most importantly we have to invest in them and in our relationships. These investments build relational capital and will serve to support our change efforts.

Accountability

Being positioned for a successful change plan requires not only data and strong relational capital, but it also requires high-minded accountability structures. In chapter 6, we covered the importance of Reciprocal Accountability and the importance of each team member being accountable to one another. When we are on our journey to change, the accountability we have toward one another will be important to our success. While the idea of reciprocal accountability serves as the foundational element of accountability, it is also necessary to ensure that the formal structures of vertical and horizontal accountability exist.

Simply put, *vertical accountability* refers to accountability within the organizational hierarchy, while *horizontal accountability* refers to accountability among peers. In 2021 the Tampa Bay Buccaneers won their second franchise championship. This championship team exemplified one of the greatest examples of the balance between vertical and horizontal accountability.

The year prior to their 2021 championship, the Buccaneers had acquired an all-star quarterback, Tom Brady, from the New England Patriots. Once Brady joined the team, he petitioned to have his old teammate, tight end Rob Gronkowski, to join him. These two players represented one of most successful quarterback-receiver duos in NFL history. Additionally, the management of the team worked to put an all-star cast of players around Tom, and to make a long story short, they had a remarkable year. This one-year turnaround was something special to watch and it brought Tampa only their second championship in franchise history.

After the team had won, the head coach, Bruce Arians, was interviewed about the team's remarkable success. His response was very telling as to why this team was so successful. In short, he explained this team was successful because the top management of the team, including Bruce Arians, hired the right players and valued their input and contributions. Arians went on to explain how he and the players worked together to manage the game plan and that he often relied on his players to provide vital information and to make key decisions.

Arians went on to share that although he was the head coach, he relied on Brady to run the offense. He let his all-star quarterback call the shots when necessary. He explained that when they had to change the game plan quickly due to real-time information, he left Brady to make the call.

Arians and Brady exemplify a *vertical accountability* structure. Brady and his teammates exemplify the *horizontal accountability structure*. These two forms of accountability, when done well, create championship teams like the 2021 Buccaneers.

In many ways, the 2021 Tampa Bay Buccaneers did everything right. They hired the right players. They all shared a common *why*. Each team member was engaged, and they all worked with one another, and for one another, to bring home the championship. Further, they had all the right structures in place, they developed the right tools to manage their game plan, and they knew how to adapt and change along the way. They had a strong team, the right tools, and they hit their target. It was something special to witness.

When organizations are able to finely tune their accountability structures the way the Buccaneers did, they are better positioned for success and are more adaptable to change. Recognizing the formal vertical and horizontal accountability structures that exist and gluing them together with a strong sense of reciprocal accountability is, as Ray Dalio put it, like playing beautiful jazz together. When we are managing our change plans, leveraging our accountability structures will lead to greater success and improved outcomes.

Calibration

Managing and leveraging change is great work. It is meaningful work. When done well, with the right people and tools, change can lead to great things for your people and your organization. But when doing so, the path is not always clear, and the future is not always easy to see. Which is why regular calibration is necessary. Moving forward along our path of change requires us to regularly reflect, use our tools, and calibrate moving forward. Using reflection tools and data analysis allows us to manage our change plan and make any necessary adjustments moving forward.

If you know much about the story of Netflix or Amazon or many of the other industrial giants, you know the way they started is not who they are today. Along the way they adjusted and adapted to change and had to recalibrate to get them moving in the right direction. This is just a simple reminder, as we close, that in all our efforts to lead it is necessary to reflect, gather information, and recalibrate to get you and your team moving toward a successful outcome.

Summary

Managing change requires us to take an aerial view of our organization and determine if our challenges are technical, behavioral or a combination of both. Aerial positioning gives us the ability to see the larger picture and examine the conditions, competencies, and cultures within our organization. This allows us to diagnose our challenges and design our change plan. Further, as we manage change, it is necessary to use diagnostic tools to help us uncover our areas of growth and possibility. Once we have gained a clear understanding, we are positioned to leverage data, accountability, and relationships to get the ball moving forward. Finally, any well devised change plan will come in contact with adversity, and when it does, it is necessary to use our knowledge of change and our tools to calibrate and adjust our plan.

Love in Action

- Have you been standing too close to the elephant? Are there areas within your organization that require an aerial perspective? Are there technical and/or behavioral challenges that you and your organization face that need examination?

  - Step back from one of your challenges and determine if the issue is technical or behavioral. Then decide if there are systems and/or too that can help.

- What tools can you use that may be useful in executing your change plan?
  - Do some research and find a problem-solving tool, a change management tool, or a project management tool that will give you structure to meeting your challenges.
- Are you able to use data, relationships, and accountability structures to move change forward?
  - When faced with a challenge, determine how you can use data, relationship, and accountability to leverage your change plan.
- In your change plan, have you left time and space for reflection and recalibration?
  - Develop a rhythm of consistency with your team and create a regular time and space for reflection, review, and calibration.

Authors Note

There is a need for high-minded servant leaders. Leaders who serve to elevate others and bring forth a common good. It is through great leadership that we will improve our homes, our communities, and our businesses. In order to do so, we must be leaders who step into the arena every day with the internal strength that has been developed by personal care and love for ourselves.

As leaders, we must take our seat of leadership with full hearts and still minds that have been intentionally designed for purposeful leadership. This requires us to be focused on creating and developing ourselves. Caring for ourselves and loving ourselves is not a recommendation—it is a requirement of our creator. We have been given an absolutely magical and awe-inspiring experience to contribute to a world that needs great leaders. In order to do so, we have to be aware that the vessel we have been given requires our attention and maintenance. We are required to work hard to care for our spirits and our bodies.

We are required to take the time to keep our vessels in tune, cared for, and mentally sharp. In doing so, we must be intentional about framing our personal narratives, and we must make sure the story we are telling with our lives is one of service and the giving of ourselves to others. That personal narrative—that is, the internal mental script—is our responsibility. It is our story to write, craft, and reinforce on a regular basis through our habits, rituals, and routines.

Our lives require us to have meaning and purpose and to understand the *why* of our existence. Knowing what we are living for and how we choose to use our lives is a critical element in living a life of meaning and fulfillment. At the foundation of who we are is our *why*, and being aware of our *why* allows us to approach our leadership stories with a high-minded sense of purpose and meaning.

Further, as leaders, it is vitally important that we are highly intentional about our own well-being. Too often I have witnessed leaders put their minds and their bodies second to the competing demands of their work. I have seen how this leaves them exhausted and misaligned. Tending to our physical bodies is of the utmost importance, and developing the habits and routines of a healthy lifestyle will only serve to make us better leaders who are energized and ready for the game. It doesn't just end with our bodies. It is also vitally important that we fill our cups with positive experiences, play, and a little fun along the way! We must make time for positivity in our lives, as it serves to fill our cups and strengthen our vitality.

Like I had mentioned at the beginning of the book, this is not intended to be a book about any particular religion; however, I do believe we are spiritual beings having a physical human experience. **It is to the extent that we align our minds and our bodies to this spiritual experience, in all areas of our lives and also within our leadership journeys, that we will live a life of high mindedness, peace, fulfillment, and meaning.** It is my hope that each of us lives in this space, where we connect deeply to our spirits and lead lives that reflect the people we want to be and the people we want to become.

When we live in this space, we bring ourselves to our seat of leadership with the sense to serve and to work hard to improve the lives of those with whom we have been entrusted. Being complete people allows us to give from our sense of fullness, and it is this sense of personal fulfillment that allows us to give to those we are leading. When we lead from a place of fulfillment, we take what we have internally and share it with our employees, our communities, and the organizations we lead.

It is from that place that we are positioned to capture the why and purpose of our work. We share with those both inside and outside the organization the importance of our work and how our work serves to contribute to the lives of others. When we lead with love, our work serves to improve and add value to human lives, and that story must be shared with the people we lead and the people we serve.

Beyond crafting and living our purpose, we must be sure to care for our people by making our organization a place where people can contribute and share their assets. A place where individual well-being is placed in high regard and where team strength is valued. The strength of our individual players is critical to the strength of our teams, and along the way each individual needs mentorship, coaching, and partnership to help sharpen their skills and build their capacities.

Caring for and loving our people is the foundation of our human experience. It is the lifeblood of our communities, our families, and our organizations. As leaders, we must be keenly aware that we are living in a spiritual realm that requires people to care for one another. This human act of love allows us to better cooperate and work together for common good and common purposes. Your leadership and mine, alike, require us to care for those we lead. It is our responsibility, through our acts of love, to create an environment that supports the human spirit and creates a space for people to become the greatest possible contributors to our world.

While loving ourselves and others is vital to our existence, we must recognize that love is, in one form, an action. *Love* is a verb. If we care deeply for our organization, we must take action to set up the systems and structures for people to thrive and be successful. Being intentional about our organizational design is an act of care. It allows people to understand their roles, contribute to the success of the team, and tap into their internal motivators.

Some final words I would like to share: Leadership matters. It is so vitally important to our lives, our families, our organizations, and our nations. High-quality leadership represents the best of ourselves and our organizations. Leading with love brings about purpose and meaning in both our lives and others. It leads to cooperation among individuals and fosters care and support. It works hard to lead people to becoming their best selves by creating an organizational culture that fosters personal motivation and fulfillment. **Ultimately, leading with love is a symbiotic act with our creator. It is our becoming the manifestation of love that we were designed to be. It is our divine role in this very temporary life.**

Love is patient, love is kind. It always protects, always trusts, always hopes, always preservers.

—1 Corinthians 13:4–7

CPSIA information can be obtained
at www.ICGtesting.com
Printed in the USA
LVHW071556090623
749338LV00004B/45